TAKE A WALK
ON THE
WILD SIDE

**FROM P-ADDICTION,
HELL AND HEARTBREAK,
TO LIFE AND A DATE WITH DESTINY**

www.wildside.com.mx

JANET BALCOMBE

Quotes taken from Streams in the Desert by L.B. Cowman updated by Jim Reimann. Copyright © 1997 by Zondervan. Used by permission of Zondervan.
www.zondervan.com

All scripture quotations are taken from the Holy Bible, New International Version®, NIV®, unless otherwise stated. Copyright ©1973, 1978, 1984, 2011 by Biblica, Inc.™ Used by permission of Zondervan. All rights reserved worldwide. www.zondervan.com The "NIV" and "New International Version" are trademarks registered in the United States Patent and Trademark Office by Biblica, Inc.™

Scripture is taken from the New King James Version®. Copyright ©1982 by Thomas Nelson, Inc. Used by permission. All rights reserved.

All quotes that are not in the public domain have been used with permission. Information on the third eye used with permission from http://kimolsen. wordpress.com/2007/08/31/opening-the-third-eye-christians-beware/

Written and designed by J. Balcombe. Edited by a complete miracle, Lissa Weight. Also edited by B. Balcombe, D. Whyman, K. Wilson, and D. Jamison. Cover design by Nicole Danswan at Ark House Press, Australia. Beautifully printed in New Zealand through Bernard Yeo at Outline Print Consultancy Ltd, Auckland.

ISBN: 978-0-473-28007-9
ISBN ebook: 978-0-473-28006-2

WSP.

Wild Side Publishing

DEDICATION

SOLI DEO GLORIA
For your glory

I saw Satan fall like lightning from heaven.
I have given you authority to trample on snakes and scorpions
and overcome all the power of the enemy;
nothing will harm you.

Luke 10:19

ஒஒ ஓஒ

CONTENTS

ACKNOWLEDGEMENTS

Mum and Dad. Wouldn't have made it without you.

Robert Glen Balcombe. No words, my brother.

Sam, my sister. For loving me, no matter what.

Roq Robert Balcombe. I'm so proud of you.

Mark. For the good years.

Josh and Danielle. For being who you are. I love you.

Marlene Bickers (nee Braggins). The brave one.

Mary Nichols. For a lifetime of love and prayer.

Erin and Sheryl Underwood. For the early days.

Trevor and Jan Yaxley. For paying the price.

Dave and Becky Price. For Growing Kids God's Way.

Sharon Thorburn. Warrior princess and bestie.

Mthunzi and Bridget Siwela. For who you are.

Noeline and Wayne Douglas. For the inspiration.

Dave and Sue. Great friends, great patience.

Kim and the bro. For putting up with us all this time.

Mark's parents, Lynn & Rae. For putting up the bail.

Phill Matthias. Sadly missed. R.I.P.

Shane. For barking at the dogs, and keeping me humble.

Gilda and Stana. For babysitting me.

Lissa Weight. For polishing God's jewel to a brilliant shine.

Sam Shosanya, Diane Jamison. For your support.

My husband and King, the God of Abraham, Isaac and Jacob,
the lover of my soul. For everything.

MAY WE NEVER

be so consumed by earning a living,

THAT WE FORGET TO LIVE,

until we have burned out the flame

THAT IS US SHINING.

there are always two paths.

— *Sharon Thorburn*

FOREWORD

*"What do you do when you've laid hold of the things
you thought would make you happy, but they became a spade
in your hand that digs a hole so deep you can't crawl out,
or see the light at the top?"*

*"I wanted to leave but was simply unable. Change, loneliness
and the unknown were scarier than the familiar."*

Step inside the pages of this book and you step inside the life of Janet Balcombe. Chapter by chapter the nightmare that became her life unfolds. You may be able to judge her, but you will never be able to forget her story. She grew the courage to face her demons, without blame or censure. Janet, the person, stands transparent and vulnerable through every page you are about to share.

This book did not emerge easily. I have heard Janet battling in the night against the darkness that threatened to penetrate her soul as she chose to expose it. I have heard her weeping over any pain she may cause her extended family by choosing total vulnerability in sharing her life with you, a world of strangers. The woman I met with the haunted eyes has walked in her freedom and found peace. She has dared to publish this book so that you can find yours.

Her book has touched my life and helped me find the courage to put down my own spade and turn. Turn the page and dare to take a walk on the wild side.

Mizpah

Sharon Thorburn Q.S.M

INTRODUCTION

Almost everyone knows someone whose life has been shattered
by bullying, addiction, adultery, bereavement, incarceration, a toxic
relationship, or even affected by the paranormal. Or maybe it's you.

Take a walk on the wild side with me and know, that even when hope
has been lost, love still whispers the promise that a life can be restored.

Be encouraged by my personal journey from hell to whole.

You are not alone.

Janet Balcombe

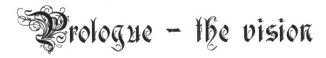

Prologue – the vision

2001

I opened the door and saw it. Like a scene straight out of The Exorcist, the Portacot defied gravity; floating in mid-air, like a sailing ship without the sea. It was moving up and down while the sides pulsated, in and out, in and out, like some macabre horror movie prop.

The scream lost traction halfway up my throat. Sweat popped along my forehead. Electricity charged the air, dragging the hair on my neck to attention. Fear overrode maternal instinct. I fled, terror at my heels, leaving my son in the cot. I knew I had witnessed evil. I could feel its icy caress. I could smell its charcoal hide. I could hear the white-cold whisper of its promises.

Turning my back on its velvet voice, I went to Mum's bedroom.

"Mum," my voice fought for freedom. Mum slept with one eye open these days. "There's something wrong in Roq's room."

It remained unspoken, but we both knew. It was ungodly. I turned to go to Roq's room with her, but Mum's hand stayed my wrist.

"No Jan, I'll handle this. Wait here."

She began praying as she headed toward Roq's room. Her voice firmed slightly as she neared his door. I heard the door open and then, silence, as the door swung shut behind her in a quiet click.

My feet took me to the kitchen, unconsciously seeking comfort from the hub of the house. I stared numbly out of the window, striving to make sense of this craziness. My surroundings had faded to grey, but the after-image was still etched on my retinas. The chill of evil clung to my skin and touched my bones. If that was a nightmare, I hoped it was over.

Slowly returning from orbit, my eyes adjusted to the darkness outside. I was seeking normalcy, but there was something different about the garden. I moved closer to the window and pushed my face against the glass. I couldn't grasp what I was seeing. It was bizarre. There was a new path winding through our lawn. In places, it was doubling back on itself like a never-ending figure of eight. Oh, God! I'm still in it. Wake up!

The path's edges were neatly finished with a brick border. An attempt had been made to pave the middle, but it was just a collection of broken pieces of brick lying on the surface. At first glance, the path looked smooth, but when you looked closely it was very rough. This was an illusion that had no end. It contained promises it couldn't deliver. My feet turned me around and took me to my room, automatically trying to distance me from the inconvenient truth, this metaphor for my life.

The static in the air made me jump, and an icy breeze touched my skin. A knowing, and a fear of the unknown curled into one. Even the hair on my face stood on end. New speakers morphed into the ceiling corners, and a chilling monotone spewed out like thick lava. The low, gravelly voice described all manner of unspeakable horrors, freezing the marrow in my bones. Everything went black. My nervous system was shutting down. My mind frantically checked every corner, looking for the escape, for some defense mechanism in which to hide.

Mounds of rubbish burned in piles by the path. I blinked again and again trying to process what I was seeing, as if my eyelids could somehow power a cognitive process. Those piles of rubbish — they weren't rubbish at all. Those were our things. Mark's and my belongings from the life we were living. From the lie I was living. The best money could buy fuelled the flames to reach higher and further into the darkness. Super-charged sparks spiralled high into the air like fiery messengers.

I'd stopped breathing. The only movement in my chest was my heart slamming into my ribs. I absorbed it all in an instant; then my eyes were drawn to him. The beast. Looking like a man, he was evil in the flesh. He had four thick, curved horns on his head. Two in front, two in the back, like giant hippo tusks. Tattooed sleeves adorned his arms. He stood too close for comfort, calmly prodding the fire. My fire.

I searched the files in my fractured brain, trying to find something to help, but I knew there was nothing. My sanity strained at its tethers. I was in hell. The remnants of a prayer wafted up on the dust from a childhood file. I picked up its trail as a drowning person clings to his rescuer. The chances of remembering it were small under the best conditions, but right now shock was setting in. On some level, I knew this was my only hope. It was the key.

"Our Father who art in heaven…"

Mum had hung a mirror on the wall with a scripture on it. Hope found a voice and my eyes searched the wall, confident I could find it. It'd been the only thing there, after all. Incredibly, the wall was now covered with irrelevant, inconsequential sayings and beliefs I'd picked up over the years and blindly held to be true.

"Better the devil you know."

"Cleanliness is next to godliness."

"It's not what you know, it's who you know."

"It's ok if you're not hurting anyone else."

"Do it to them before they do it to you."

"God helps those who help themselves."

"The power comes from within."

"You create your own reality."

"Whoever dies with the most toys wins."

"The end justifies the means."

Pictures of things I held dear that had no eternal value also crowded the wall, more useless crap, things that would turn to chaff and be blown away in the coming fire. What you put into the mind comes out in a life. There was no trace of the scripture.

Desperate, I strained to remember the rest of the prayer. It was all I had. Standing in the face of obscenity, I was flooded with the knowledge that

God's power is the ultimate power. But I still felt God wasn't listening, and I was unworthy of his help. I stood on the edge of the abyss between God and me, with no idea how to cross, evil snapping at my heels. I remained grasping at straws in the darkness, my mouth ajar as I stared into the flames.

Be still and know that I am God.
Psalm 46:10

I awoke, my scream unborn, in a pool of cold sweat. Terror-induced rigor mortis stopped me from pulling the blankets over my head. Was it a dream, or had it happened? Had it come from outside or inside of me? And what was that stuff about God? I didn't want God. Anything but God!

Eventually, my feet responded to the command. Move! They reluctantly covered the familiar path to Roq's room. I stopped in front of his door, wondering what I'd see when I opened it. My hand stretched out and pushed it slowly open. I forced myself to breathe. The crib was on the floor. Good. I snatched my sleeping child by the scruff of the neck and dived back into bed like a rugby player over the line. I'd experienced something unnatural, but very real. I was shaken to the core. Unable to turn the light off and give heed to another reign of darkness, it was a long time before my eyes closed.

Morning arrived. The frosting on the lawn ignored the weak winter sun. I dragged my weary bones to the kitchen and fell into a dining room chair, and as I stared vacantly out the window, I frowned as something had nudged my consciousness. The new path was gone.

The night came flooding back. Memory laden with the filth that I'd met last night was harsh in the cold light of day. Filth that Mum had confronted in my stead, without question. Adrenaline rudely unleashed for such an early hour left me trembling. Mum was standing at the sink, savouring the last of the morning peace before the day slowly but surely picked up its pace.

"I had a dream last night," I said tonelessly.

"Mmm?" Mum said, cool green eyes scanning my face.

"I dreamed Roq's cot was going up and down in the air, and the sides were breathing in and out. There was such a feeling of menace. I've never felt such terror. Such despair."

Mum slowly placed her bone china mug on the bench and turned towards me. Her quiet authority filled the kitchen.

"When I got up this morning I didn't know you'd taken Roq to your bed in the night. I went in to check on him and was struck by the chill in the room. When I rested my hands on the cot it felt so cold I thought it was wet, but it wasn't. Something had been in the room, and I think that maybe... "

Mum's voice drifted off, and she turned her gaze to the window. The remnants of heaviness fled, and my senses stood to attention.

"Maybe? Maybe what, Mum?"

"A presence. I'll bless the room tonight."

My toes curled. Tonight? But we have to be here all day, I thought.

"I think that maybe you weren't dreaming. That God pulled back the spiritual curtain and showed you something. I think that maybe, you had a vision."

The hair on my scalp reached for height, once again.

In a dream, in a vision of the night, when deep sleep falls on people as they slumber in their beds, he may speak in their ears and terrify them with warnings, to turn them from wrongdoing and keep them from pride, to preserve them from the pit, their lives from perishing by the sword.
Job 33:15-18

ৡৡ ৡৡ

You will never do anything in this world without courage.
It is the greatest quality of the mind next to honour.
Aristotle

ৡৡ ৡৡ

1. Crossroads

1981

George Bernard Shaw said youth is wasted on the young, and I can see his point. It's easy to fall into the 'what ifs', and wonder how things could have been different; but the fact is, I wouldn't change a thing in my life. My journey has led me to know real truth, and real freedom, and I wouldn't have it any other way.

It was just an ordinary school day, the day my world fell apart for the very first time. Admittedly school had been a bit weird lately. I just couldn't shake the knot in my gut. Things hadn't been the same since a couple of girls had started hanging out with me and my bestie. I liked them, but I began to get the feeling they didn't like me that much anymore. After a while I was being not-so-subtly excluded from the group. I didn't want to be excluded from the group, because the group included my best friend since we were five years old. I was a little slow getting with the programme, so they gave me a nudge.

Dumping my bag on the floor and collapsing onto my bed, I kicked off my shoes. Like most teenagers after a day at school, I was ravenously hungry. I unzipped my bag to drag out my lunch-box before heading to the kitchen. My hands connected with a bunch of paper I didn't recognise. I pulled out what looked like a booklet made from several sheets of refill stapled together. *What?* How did this get in my bag? What was it? The title was simply one word: 'HER', and underneath was a skillfully hand-drawn portrait of my face. A surreal feeling crept over me as my mind tried to process what I was seeing. Cold fingers of fear and shock began to claw at my skin. I turned the page and saw that three authors had contributed a couple of pages each. I began to read. By the time I had finished, Janet Balcombe had suffered mortal injuries, and was bleeding out on the inside. The character assassination took six pages and systematically listed every single thing the group hated about me. I had been judged, and found wanting.

If a group of people that I had counted as my friends had invested such time and effort putting this manifesto together, it must surely be true. There were three of them, and only one of me. They had to be right. It was written. I was unacceptable and unaccepted. I wasn't hungry anymore. As I sat staring numbly into a black abyss, still holding the booklet when Mum came into the room and looked at me. An avalanche of shame buried me and I automatically hid the booklet under the pillow.

"What's that?"

"Nothing."

Mum left the room suspicious, sure I was hiding something naughty. At the first possible moment I carried out a covert mission to the incinerator to destroy the evidence of my failure as a human being. The paper writhed and burned, but the words were etched on the stone of my heart. I was irrevocably changed in that moment as I pulled up at the signpost of a major life detour.

At school, when my art teacher addressed me daily as *'that Balcombe idiot,'* I just couldn't brush it off anymore. The trouble was, I kept waking up every morning. I wished I didn't. The trouble was, I had to keep going to school. I wished I didn't. The trouble was me, or so I thought. I was a very difficult teenager after that. Hurt, angry, confused. Empty. Lonely. And the most annoying thing was, everywhere I went, there I was.

Defense mechanisms were my friends. Hardness. Toughness. I invented a new person to be. *The Rebel.* The one who couldn't be hurt because she didn't care. I was torn between needing to be accepted and not caring. *Anaesthetic.* When I left school I dulled the pain with drink, cigarettes and drugs. This gave me the confidence to function socially and tricked myself into believing I was worthy of the space I was taking up. *The Mask.* The makeup went on with a shovel and I conjured an appearance that approached some paradigm of beauty portrayed by the cultural authority — the media. *Avoid Females.* I concluded all women were bitches and employed avoidance behaviour line with a social anxiety disorder.

For our struggle is not against flesh and blood, but against the rulers, against the authorities, against the powers of this dark world and against the spiritual forces of evil in the heavenly realms. *Ephesians 6:12*

Making my move to Dargaville to board and work, I found a place with an adorable elderly lady.

"I don't usually take in girls; I prefer boys, they're less complicated," she said.

I completely understood. Me too. I valued her vote of confidence and didn't disappoint her. She didn't flinch at the Goth-punk outfits I crafted at her kitchen table. She comforted me the best she could when they weren't very well received in the small country town. But then, neither was anything I did.

There were a couple of girls I got on well with, and I made friends with a local band because one of the guys was from Ruawai. He was nearly as old as my Dad, and we were just mates. Most of the other guys were engaged, but their girlfriends didn't go to band practices. Their practice shed was just behind my place, and my friend invited me, and so I went from time-to-time and even took my boyfriend. Word soon got around town that I was a slut. Upon arrival at the pub on a Friday night, I heard the murmur sweep around the patrons like a Mexican wave.

"The bitch is here."

"Slut."

I was done with Dargaville. However, it takes more than simply moving towns to outrun the schemes of the evil one.

꩜

The majestic Phoenix Palm held a silent vigil over the hotel nestled in the shadow of the Hunua Ranges. My friend Sian and I warmed up in front of the fire. The drinks were all rolling into one, as were our words. It was nice to have a girlfriend to have a few drinks with, a rare treat. I'd had a bad run. Sian was a nice, decent girl. No wonder her mother didn't like me.

"Far out, that was terrible about that dealer the other night. Did you hear what happened?" Sian asked. We worked together at a merchant bank in Queen Street, Auckland. She was in settlements while I was in foreign exchange doing data input for the dealing team, aka The Terriers.

"Yea, they were out drinking. He had a bad fall. That was it." I said.

"Man, that's awful. That could easily have been one of us," Sian said. It was true.

"I know. We're just as bad for getting wasted," I said. The dealer's death had shocked me as badly as anything could in my emotionally dead, heavily medicated state. It was too close to home. I had my own reminder of a night out gone wrong.

The thief comes only to steal and kill and destroy.
John 10:10

We worked hard and played hard. It was a high-stress game. We drank every night at work in the free bar until we were off our faces. It wasn't long before we'd destroyed the bar for the last time, and were banned.

At nineteen, I was already a binge-drinking alcoholic. I prided myself on not needing to drink every day, thinking that disqualified me from being an alcoholic. I was wrong. We found a new drinking hole, the Regent Hotel wine bar, simply because it was the nearest place to work, and we didn't want to waste time en route. However, it wasn't long before we were banned from there too.

"How's your foot now? You can wear a shoe finally; so that's good," said Sian, looking down at the hoof in question.

"Yea, it's getting there. I can wear a shoe now, but it gets sore sometimes. It's numb where the heel had to grow back."

My foot had been incarcerated for months in a cast with a window to dress the wound while I healed, or re-heeled.

"You know, Danny offered me $200 compensation for running my foot over. I didn't take it. There's no one to blame but my stupid self," I said.

"That was nice of him though, eh?" she said.

I was getting out of the car, and my foot had been caught under the tyre of Danny's car when he dropped a patch. I just felt a bump and pulled away my foot as soon as I could, but it had already been ground into the road a fair bit before I could free it. It had happened so fast. I was shocked at my stocking, ripped to the worst; it looked like a shark attack. Then I saw my foot. It was a shark attack! It was chewed to the bone on the inside, from my toes to my heel, right up to my ankle. Almost half my heel was gone. Just gone. Chewed up and spat out by the cold, uncalculating tarseal. I poked my foot through the middle of the seats to the front to show the guys, because I was all out of words.

"Look at this," I said calmly, taking advantage of my shock. This was a skill that would stand me in good stead.

"Ahh!" they screamed. Danny drove straight to the hospital. They stayed with me, faces ashen as the nurse cleaned the lumps of stone out of the raw meat with what looked like a toothbrush. Pain relief was out of the question. I'd had too much alcohol. However, the shark attack had sobered me right up, and I felt everything intensely.

Danny's face said it all. He felt worse. Daily hospital visits ate his lunch hours until I was released. Nine long months passed before I could wear a shoe, and years passed until the shoe stopped torturing me. My drinking was a worry, and I was getting sick of it, but had no idea how to stop. I just couldn't see myself not drinking. Nope, I just couldn't see how it could work, I thought as I chugged back another beer. Drinking was part of my new identity, my anaesthetic, courage and release. It was my social scaffolding.

"Far out! Did you see how many people were packed into the viewing gallery yesterday?" Sian said. "It must have been a record."

"For sure, it was hilarious. They couldn't stop staring at me," I roared, laughing. Not one to dwell on unpleasantries, I was a master of denial. Sian had seen me when I'd first come for my interview. Wearing a soft grey jumper and a skirt, my conservative outfit was perfect for interviews, and my medium brown hair was blow-waved into an impressive 80s ski-ramp.

"Do you have computer experience?"

"Oh yes," I lied, knowing I was a quick learner. Heck, it was 1985. I was eighteen. They'd only just invented computers then, but I was always up for a challenge. That was probably the one thing I liked about myself.

"Well, that's good. You know this is a sole-charge position, although we'll give you two weeks on-the-job training. When can you start?" There couldn't have been many applicants.

"Next week, I just have to move my gear from Dargaville. I've got a flat in Herne Bay I can move into with my brother," I beamed.

"Good. We'll see you then," confirmed my new employer.

Wow! I'm an Aucklander now. I might treat myself to a little makeover. I'd tried a Goth punk approach in Dargaville, which I liked, even though it hadn't been very well received. The following week I arrived for work, but I don't think they recognised me. My makeover was complete. The hair was a classic short Billy Idol, sapphire blue with blonde tiger stripes died into the razor cutting on the left ear, finishing at the back. Permed curls overhung the razor cut, peaking low front and back. A custom slashed black t-shirt revealed a fluoro layer. Black lace fingerless gloves punctuated the top half. Enter the micro-mini. Was it a skirt, shorts, or a belt? Let's go with a skirt. Three studded belts finished the bottom half, along with fishnet stockings and black lace-up boots.

Oh, and the make-up. Quite striking. Heavy purple eyeshadow streaking right out to the ends of the eyebrows adorned the metallic pearl base coat. Black eyeliner sealed the bottom lid, and chunky mascara coated the eyelashes and eyebrows. Pancake foundation two shades too dark, shovelled on, provided sufficient camouflage. A subtle flourish of blusher and pink pearl lipstick to finish, and I was done! Didn't want to overdo it.

"They didn't know what to look at first," I said to Sian, "the hair, the make-up or the clothes!" We laughed hard.

Every time the market moved, which was often, members of the public poured into the viewing gallery to watch the dealers in action. My desk was one of the cubicles in the main dealing desk, so they got extra bang for their buck. It wasn't long before word spread around town about the 'apparition' in the FX department, and they came to see it with their own eyes. The cool ones laughed. The superior ones' noses lifted a couple of centimetres so they could peer down it at me in disgust.

We turned at the rumble of Harley's, the call of the wild. "Look, here come Leon and Greg," said Sian. The two guys we'd been chatting to earlier returned.

"You girls want to come to a party?" Leon shouted over the dull roar of the public bar, nodding to his bike out front. He didn't have a spare helmet that I could see. They seemed nice, nothing not to like. I checked Sian for a reaction and dragged hard on my cigarette. She shrugged 'whatever.'

"Got spare helmets?" I asked. Safety first. "I'm not going anywhere without a helmet," I told him flatly.

The trigger replayed the last conversation with my only brother for the thousandth time. The 12th of October 1986, the day Robert had met his maker at twenty-four years of age. His words met me from the birthday party, "I don't want to be the twelfth."

"What?" my voice echoed through the passage of time.

"Eleven people have already been killed this long weekend, and I don't want to be the twelfth. I'm only having one beer tonight."

The cryptic statement piqued my attention amidst the happy hum of friends and family. Unwelcome fingers of premonition touched his soft heart. Denial touched mine. I put it down to my sober brother 'having a moment.' He was a thinker. I wasn't.

Later, Robert's Suzuki hummed smoothly beneath Robert and Marlene as they cruised down Titirangi Road, nearing home. Spotting Marlene's brother on the footpath, Robert pulled over.

"Hey, Jay! I'll drop Marlene home then come back for you," said Robert.

"Yea ok, thanks!" Jay said, waving Robert and Marlene off.

The headlights of the oncoming delivery van veered and bounced at the hands of the drunk approaching. At the last minute, the murderer remembered his turnoff and hauled his van across the road in front of the newlyweds. The bike bucked as it hit the side of the covered van. Robert's spleen ruptured. Marlene's brother heard the mighty smash. His heart lurched. He ran.

As Marlene skidded along the road on her back in her grey leather miniskirt and new boots, the full weight of the GCX 1100cc bike crashed on top of her. Pelvis shattered. Graceful hands smashed. Soft stomach tore; womb bled out on the road. Oncoming traffic bathed the bike wreckage and motionless bundles on the road in light, highlighting the terrible scene.

Jay stopped, paralysed, struggling to believe his eyes. He ran to his sister, throwing the bike off her as if it were weightless, without even realising what he was doing. He only saw his sister.

"Marlene? *MARLENE! Oh God, oh God!*"

Police secured the scene. Jason watched mutely as paramedics persuaded Marlene's heart with defibrillation paddles as she lay where she had fallen, the same heart that had been beating less than five minutes earlier. The killer snaked his way off into the night, concluding Marlene and Robert's nine-month marriage and shattering two families in a split-second. No stranger to hit-and-run, he fled to save his slimy skin.

My fingers tightened on my glass, and hot anger flared after raw pain. Why do bad things happen to good people? Where was God when my family lay bleeding on the road?

The same place I was when My Son hung, bleeding on the cross. Right there with him.

Ok, I don't get it.

You will.

Sian's pretty face came into focus as she nudged me from my reverie. Sian had been a friend to me when I'd first started work, a brave move. Loyalty hid behind a kind and gentle exterior. She nodded toward Leon.

"I haven't got a spare helmet," Leon said lamely.

I skulled the last of my warm beer and slammed the glass down. "I'll get one," I said dully, mashing my cigarette into the ashtray. Now reality was starting to bite. I got up, remembering a whole line of bikes right outside the pub's front windows. Most had helmets hanging from the handlebars.

"I'll get a helmet. Frickin' idiots, can't do anything for themselves," I muttered. Anger festered and bubbled. It seemed, no matter how wasted I got, I could never forget. Grief and pain had laid a thick gravestone over the hole in my heart. Recklessness danced on top.

Trolling up and down the line of bikes, I looked for a decent helmet. Heck, might as well grab a pair of gloves while I'm at it. The impromptu retail therapy perked me up a little, adding a little more length to my very short wick. Hmm, black or black? I helped myself to the gang member's gear as they watched me through the glass. Sian, Leon, and Greg were speechless. Pretending they didn't know me, they tried to stay out of view of the bikers.

"Hey Sian, want a helmet?" I was feeling generous. Her Eve's apple darted up, then down as she tried to answer but couldn't think of anything to say.

"Um."

Dark eyes collectively watched me don the helmet and gloves.

"Hurry up then!" I barked at the others. They snapped into action, keen to make a getaway asap. I set the two beer bottles down in between Leon and me as we rode off down the long driveway. Straight off, his riding style wasn't filling me with confidence. In fact, he either couldn't ride for shit or he was drunker than I was. Probably both. At the end of the drive, attempting to turn onto the road, Leon dropped the bike. It's possible he was put off by the concept of transporting an outlaw with a price on her head. Was he guilty by association?

"Now that doesn't surprise me," I thought, as we sprawled in slow motion on the road to the ambience of screeching metal on tar seal. The beer bottles smashed and harpooned my thigh. I got up and swore at the guy. "F*#@ you, mate!" I snarled, pulling a nasty shard of glass from the short but deep cut.

"I'm walking!" I shouted over my shoulder and stalked off, thumb out, stumbling through Greg and Sian's exhaust fumes as they roared off, unaware. Silently the gang mobilised. A car was dispatched to pick me up as I hitched down the road, helmet in hand. When they pulled up, I didn't recognise any of them because I hadn't even seen them in the first place. Happy a ride had come along so soon, I jumped in the car. The guys seemed nice and friendly.

"Want to go to a party?"

"Ok," I said, squeezing into the car, still clutching the helmet. I wondered whether it was the same party we'd heard about, and whether I'd catch up with her there. We drove deep into unknown countryside until I was very lost. Merging into the frenetic crowd in the marquee, it wasn't long before I saw Sian's auburn spirals bobbing to the beat.

"Hey, that dickhead couldn't ride for shit!" I laughed.

"Yea, I wondered what happened to you," she smiled, scanning the crowd. "This is a massive party."

"Yea, it must be a twenty-first." Bikes and cars filled half a paddock. The isolated farm had one road in and one road out, a dead end. Music pulsed through the atmosphere with no neighbours to complain. The whole marquee was a mosh pit. Someone near me planted an elbow sharply into my side. It hurt, but I put it down to an accident — it was easy enough to do in a crowd like this. But again, another hard blow, then another. I tried to see who it was, but couldn't tell. No one was looking. Deciding I was imagining it, I had just started to relax again when yet another hard blow landed, really hurting.

That was it. I'd had enough. After the stuffiness of the marquee, the fresh country air was sobering and the sky, gorgeous. The magnificence of infinite stars shining like diamonds on a velvet sky in an ever-expanding universe took my breath away.

The heavens declare the glory of God; the skies proclaim the work of his hands. Day after day they pour forth speech; night after night they reveal knowledge. *Psalm 19:1-2*

I released myself to the night sky, finding unconscious comfort in something much larger than myself.

Deep calls unto deep. *Psalm 42:7*

Suddenly I felt very small and lost. No plan, just blowing from place to place like a leaf on the winter wind? Yea. Well, that's depressing, tragic in fact. Ugly waves of despair met me in the dark hour. I couldn't enter the bitter world of my heart long enough to figure out what I wanted from life and there were walls and doors that stopped me even entering some parts. Fuelled by denial on all fronts I advanced mechanically into no-man's land, no more than a meat puppet responding to the hard taskmasters of emotion, addiction and neediness.

I tried to remember what my dreams and aspirations had been. Once upon a time there had been a tiny ballerina dancing around on my little girl's stage; then a cowgirl riding her black stallion off into the wild blue yonder with her posse. And later there had been an author penning literary offerings; however, somewhere along the line I'd given up on myself. I'd witnessed the slow death of my dreams, attended their burial, and settled for survival, along with most of mankind.

> **Every man dies, but not every man truly lives.**
> *William Wallace*

My feet were moving and so I walked, blown on a phantom wind, lost in mental misery. When my focus finally turned outward, I was in pitch darkness. No streetlights lit the way. I found myself in a dark paddock with the creepy feeling of being watched. I turned to face a gang of bikers silhouetted against the glow of the party. Silently, with one mind, they encircled me. Too late I realised my mistake. I'd played right into their hands walking out into the night by myself. Sian hadn't even noticed me go.

The big one came forward.

"You took my helmet, you dumb bitch," he spat. Heavy brows merged into one.

"No I didn't!" I said, feigning innocence.

Without warning, he lashed out. Heavy rings connected with my head, one blow knocking me down. I sprang up, hardly even touching the ground, feeling no pain. Adrenaline and cortisol charged my bloodstream.

"You took the helmet. We saw you!" His arms hung at his sides like a gunfighter at a showdown, his weight moved from foot to foot.

"No! No, I didn't! It wasn't me! Honest!" I pleaded.

The lightning punch struck again, slamming me to the ground. I bounced back up. My denials seemed to strangely confuse him even though he'd seen my crime with his own eyes. The guys were enjoying the entertainment. My ears were singing but still, no pain. Survive at all costs. Brain in overdrive; I was desperate to hatch a plan.

A girl stepped up keen to have a go. Automatically I lashed out, hitting her first. I hit her again and again, not giving her a chance. Anger and pain found an outlet. Eventually, I realised, "Oh no, maybe I'll get payback for hitting her," but I needn't have worried. They didn't care about her at all. She retreated into the circle of clones. Mono-brow stepped up again, resuming the blows to my head. This was getting old. I decided I'd had enough and wanted to go now.

"How on earth am I going to get out of this?" I wondered miserably. Then it became very simple. I wanted to leave, so I started walking. As in a dream I walked away. The circle parted and the eyes watched me go. Walking toward the darkness and a line of parked cars I could feel twenty pairs of eyes drilling into my back. I desperately wondered what to do next. Hoping I'd gone far enough to be hidden in the darkness I ducked behind a car and waited. Heart pounding, I couldn't comprehend what had just taken place. This nightmare was real. I crouched, trying to make myself invisible, to cease to exist, wondering how it could possibly end well.

"What are you doing?" a guy appeared, startling me.

"Nothing. Waiting."

"Oh," he said, as if I'd just made perfect sense. "Do you want to wait in the car? I'll wait with you," he said kindly. He seemed nice. I didn't know what else to do.

"Ok."

Understanding dawned and I realised my mistake. It was the car I'd arrived in. The helmet was still on the floor.

"Why are those guys after you?" he asked. His gentle concern weakened my resolve. I confided in him.

"I took their helmet."

"So it was you, bitch!" he snarled, lunging at me.

I had a choice. Quick, or dead? I chose quick. I punched and kicked my way out of the car. He had an iron grip on my sleeve. I slipped out of my jacket in a pirouette and sprinted, leaving him holding the empty garment. I ran and ran further into the darkness and didn't stop. The darkness was now my friend. My lifeline. I was desperate to get out of line of sight, to get low and hide in the grass until they left. After some distance, I changed direction to lose them.

I ran out of paddock and fell into a deep drain. The water was freezing, but it didn't matter. I was gutted that I'd lost my new leather jacket and the money in the pocket. Ok, I can wait it out here. The bass from the sound system in the marquee reverberated through space. Sian would be dancing and laughing in the crowd. Amazing how two people could have such polar experiences on a night out together. I was no innocent victim, however. My dilemma stemmed from questionable choices and a lack of moral fibre, once again. Nothing new there. Oh well, at least I was safe for now.

My heart rate slowed as I rested and waited, confident I just needed to wait it out until the bikers left. Wrong. My heart dropped. I watched in disbelief as my hunters began combing the paddock with flashlights. I heard a dog barking and panting. They were methodically searching the area in front of me and the distance between us was closing. There was no way they wouldn't find me, if they just kept going. Maybe I should make a run for it along the road. No. It was a dead end. Oh my God.

Headlights patrolled the driveway and only exit. I realised they weren't the giving-up types. They were the raping and murdering types. There was no way out. Even if I managed to stay hidden all night, the sun would eventually rise and expose me. The cut in my leg was filled with muddy water. My despair was complete. I wished with all my heart I were at home, safe and sound. Oh, for a quiet life. For one so reckless, I was sure fighting hard to stay alive. I didn't care if I died, but it had to be on my terms. Not theirs. Early signs of sunrise stirred in the east. Fresh panic swelled. My cover was evaporating.

"Can I wait with you?" said a voice in the darkness.

A young guy's face appeared next to me in the drain.

What? You've got to be joking. I couldn't begin to understand how he'd got there. What next? What was this; another trap? I mean if he was here with me now he must have seen the whole thing unfold. He must be one of them. The sanest possibility was that I'd lapsed into psychosis and was imagining it. I was out of options. I looked at him. He seemed really young and quite genuine and I'd been such a good judge of character so far.

"Ok."

We waited half an hour or so watching the cars on dawn patrol. Our eyes bugged and breathing stopped as the flashlight came so close, then miraculously turned and went away just metres before the big reveal.

"That was close," breathed my drain friend. I wasn't speaking.

"I have a car. If we make it to the car, I can get you out," he said. Could be a trap, but I didn't have any choice. We waited and watched and chose our moment.

"Now," he whispered. I blindly followed, trusting him with my life. He quickly unlocked his car, and I hurled myself on the floor, done caring about traps.

The sun peeped over the horizon as we drove out the gate undetected. I'd never seen the guy before, and I never saw him again.

The universe had been kind to me.

> For I know the plans I have for you, plans to prosper you and not to harm you, plans to give you hope and a future.
> *Jeremiah 29:11*

୬୭୧ ୬୧୬

2. Life changer

1990

Monday morning. I was slowly waking up. One day wasn't long enough for the recovery I needed. I felt bad. There was that feeling again. Shame. Shame from being so wasted, heightened by not knowing what had happened. Who I'd offended, who I'd slept with, what I'd lost.

The thought of another week of work was intolerable. My chest felt like a horse had kicked it under the weight of the fifty or sixty cigarettes I'd ingested over the last few days.

Remnants of a conversation I didn't care to remember drifted in with Adie's face. My beautiful friend's voice carried her concern through the noise of the nightclub crowd.

"Janet, you're getting violent when you drink these days. I'm scared of you when you're like this."

She rubbed her arm where I'd lashed out at her. There was no reply. Where do you start? It was too hard to discuss. I was an alcoholic, but drinking was a mere symptom of much larger issues. Issues that couldn't be helped by Alcoholics Anonymous meetings. My life revolved around drinking; I didn't know any other way. Alcohol insulated me against reality. Sooner or later I'd have to face up to some ugly truths, but right now that was impossible.

Dragging myself out of bed, I lurched to the shower. My head was splitting. I melted into the steamy cocoon where I often stayed until the water went cold. The humid air loosened the fresh layers of tar in my lungs. I bent double coughing, trying to free evil, sticky rubber bands. I exhaled nicotine death. Stars floated in front of my eyes. I was sick. Sick at heart. Sick for which there was no pill. Sick of my life, sick of myself. I needed anaesthetic. I needed identity. I needed truth. Alcoholism had stalked our family for generations, gathering intensity en route. Its roots went deep.

The warm shower soothed. Understanding dawned. I wasn't going to make it to my forties the way I was going. I had to give up drinking while I still could. I'd had enough. My photo album told the story of a life spent boozing, smoking, and talking crap. Apart from that, nothing else ever happened. Oh, that's a party at so-and-so's place; this is at what-zit's place, that one's at my place. And that's John with his head down the toilet. It was *so darn boring.*

I decided. That's it. I'm giving up. But I wasn't going to tell anyone in case I couldn't. I'd just do it.

Reaching for my towel, I dug deep for the intestinal fortitude to get myself to work. An executive secretary at a major trading bank in Auckland, I'd already had a few warnings about my long lunches by now. Sometimes I didn't roll back to work until four thirty in the afternoon. The girls and I were going to the Masonic Tavern for a drink tonight. Oh, no! I panicked. Should I cancel? No. I wanted to give up drinking now so I could still enjoy going out with my friends and have a good time.

Drying my face, I dreaded what came next. Steeling myself, I faced my reflection. I hated my face without make-up. I hated looking into my eyes at the stranger who lived there. I hated myself. The boring routine of applying make-up and getting ready numbed my mind every day, but the concept of not painting on my flimsy identity was unthinkable.

At school, I hid behind humour, and still did a bit, but make-up was my real hiding place. Bracing myself, I faced my reflection. I saw a pasty, featureless blob. I was quite simply the most repugnant person alive without make-up. The distortion of the image I saw was like looking into a circus mirror. I saw myself as hideous, in the way the anorexic sees herself as fat. I would nearly faint if someone saw me without make-up, which didn't happen often. I made sure of that.

Smoothing on moisturiser and eye cream felt nice. Ok, I'm getting there.

Foundation and concealer created the palette for my matte painting. Like an animator creating a character, modelling, texturing, lighting, the android became human. Growing up around beautiful people, I'd fallen into the comparison trap which leads to disaster one way or another, inferiority or pride, or swinging wildly between both. I contracted ugly-duckling disease. As a young person, my budding identity was crushed before it could even fully flower. Rejection reinforced the lies. I was grotesque. I was a bad friend.

I strained under the pressure from media to be gorgeous. What was the point in living, if you weren't beautiful? And no matter how hard I tried, why couldn't I ever be beautiful enough? The more I focused on the outside, the uglier the inside became. Pulling a classic Muriel's Wedding name change when I left home, the old identity was discarded for a new one. Jan became Janet. Soft became hard. Plain became mysterious (or something else entirely). Naïve became streetwise. Innocent became corrupt.

Instead of looking inside or to the one who made me, I looked to others for meaning, inspiration, and happiness. But as Led Zeppelin noted, no matter what I strove to change, the song remained the same.

⁘⁙⁘

I saw the roses falling from our fingers onto Robert's coffin, and the tears falling from our eyes. Ashes to ashes, dust to dust; the old Matakohe Church watched solemnly from the background, the same church where we had gathered to celebrate Marlene and Robert's wedding just nine months earlier. My emotions were clubbed into submission with a fistful of Valium, but still, despair blossomed. It should have been me.

Robert was smart, quiet, and kind. A trace of cynicism smudged my face as I remembered how disappointed Robert's teachers had been when I appeared at school, quickly smashing expectations I'd be like him; a star student. Ha! I had to work hard just to be average. One teacher addressed me daily as 'that Balcombe idiot.' That idiot without a name.

Robert had a wife, a future, and a great head on his shoulders. I was the black sheep, recklessly traversing the slippery slopes of substance abuse and wild living. Instant gratification my only motivation, I had no ambition and no goals, just a smart mouth and nothing of value to say.

It was a no-brainer. I wished I'd had the choice. Take me instead. It seems only the good die young.

Unless a kernel of wheat falls to the ground and dies, it remains only a single seed. But if it dies, it produces many seeds. *John 12:24*

Eighty miles away Marlene lay comatose in her sterile intensive care unit as her new husband was laid to rest. Finally, her eyelids flickered. Daylight touched the ruptured blood vessels that were her eyes. Everything hurt. Slowly she tried to move, and failed. 'Oh no, my legs don't work anymore,' she thought, dreamily.

Trying to see out of blood-red eyes wasn't really working. She'd been through hell, and this was just the beginning. A flat spot now graced her cornea where it had hit the helmet. Six broken ribs, collapsed lungs, broken jaw, head trauma, hands smashed. Stomach ripped open, womb torn, pelvis crushed; it was probably quicker to say what wasn't wrecked. Marlene had taken seven pints of blood before the bleeding stopped. She had died three times and had been revived with defibrillation paddles at the scene, in the ambulance, at hospital.

Realising her own injuries, Marlene just knew. Robert couldn't have survived. Marlene's Mum had become one with the chair next to the bed. No stranger to pain herself, she resisted the desire to squeeze her daughter's hand.

"Can't move legs."

"Oh sweetie." Relief, love and anguish washed over Marlene's mother. "They've had to give you drugs to stop you moving. You're too broken."

"What?" Marlene croaked.

"You were in an accident a week ago. I'm sorry."

"Robert?"

Marlene's mother wept. No goodbyes. He's gone. Broken. Husbandless. Surreal. Marlene's heart felt no pain. Marlene's heart felt nothing at all for a long, long time.

Until she chose Robert's headstone.

There was a scar on yonder mountainside,
gashed out where once the cruel storm had trod;
A barren, desolate chasm, reaching wide
across the soft green sod.

Streams in the Desert, June 22

❦

The rubber was about to meet the road. Walking up to the bar at the Masonic Tavern, I panicked. Hours of mindless drinking echoed in the stale air. What am I going to drink? I hadn't thought it through. I didn't have a plan. The floor dropped away beneath my feet; the fetid atmosphere was devoid of oxygen. Struggling not to faint, I looked away and breathed deeply while the girls bought their drinks. Coke? Too sweet. Orange juice? Too acidic. Iced water? That's it. Whew. Why didn't I think this through before I got here?

I took a mental jaywalk the minute I sat down, bored right from the start. Distracted by internal dialogue, it was hard to engage in the present moment. Reality was brutal. This was alien territory. Chain-smoking, I looked hard to find my comfort zone. My mental explorations uncovered a very high shelf. Ok. This is where I'd put things I wasn't allowed anymore, too high to reach without a ladder. I mentally climbed the ladder, placed alcohol on the shelf and descended. It was now out of my line of sight. The theory was good, but the way I was panicking, my heroic choice was already sorely tested.

"Hey Janet, aren't you drinking? Are you ok?" asked Adie.

"Yea I'm ok. Just don't feel like it," I said.

"Oh," said Adie, a little lost for words. I was still scaring her. There'd never been a problem the hair of the dog couldn't fix. A new void now existed. The law of physics demands voids must be filled.

"I've got some smoke. Anyone coming outside for a joint?" asked one of the girls.

"Yea, I'm in," without thinking I jumped at the chance to blur the edges. And so the void was filled, and one addiction was replaced with another.

❦

Mechanical beeps punctuated the antiseptic silence. Marlene lay perfectly still, perfectly quiet. It had been a week since her world had stopped so abruptly; she'd been thrown off. She'd made it out of intensive care alive. Watching. Listening. Thinking. She would come to know her room in the ward well. Lucid thought had returned now Marlene was off pain relief and immobilising meds. Pain was her closest companion, her body one long silent scream. Nurses had just turned her over, as was the half-hourly ritual since her lungs had collapsed. No small thing for one so broken. Cuss words rang through the ward every thirty minutes like a chime clock, night and day.

Soft white shoes padded in and pulled up next to Marlene. "Good morning, sweetheart," called the cheery nurse as she adjusted the drip. "I'll be back in five to do your observations," and she swished out again.

Her body-scream peaked as Marlene's bed moved under the weight of someone sitting on it. Strange, she hadn't heard anyone come in. Then she saw him. Robert sat on the side of her bed in jeans and a t-shirt. He looked at her with loving tenderness.

Marlene's heart raced. She blinked. He was still there.

"Do you know how much I love you?" he asked.

"Yes," she answered, her gut wrenching. "I love you, too."

"You'll be all right," he said with a secret smile.

Marlene's eyes brimmed. Her heart swelled with love and pain. The horribly cheerful nurse bustled back into the room to do the observations. Marlene's heart dropped. He was gone.

꧁꧂

It was Meg's birthday. My lovely, down-to-earth friend worked at the Shakespeare Tavern in Albert Street, pulling pints. The workday dragged on sluggishly. Finally, I rocked up to the Shakespeare. Meg chatted to a guy in a voluminous white business shirt as she put a pint down in front of him.

"Hey, Meg!" I smiled. "Happy birthday, mate!"

"Hey Janet, thanks. This is a mate of mine, Mark," Meg said, looking at the big guy. He looked pretty pleased with himself. I couldn't imagine why.

I ordered iced water and sparked up a cigarette. I didn't like him. He looked like a pen pusher. I didn't like pen pushers.

"Gid'ay," he said with a cheesy grin. I reeled back as a shaft of light pinged off a gold tooth. Liking what he saw, he set out to dazzle me with his conversation. Everything he said made me mad.

"You're just a pen pusher, and I hate pen pushers," I said. With that, he took off his tie, then his shirt and strutted around the bar. People stopped. The hum of the bar dropped to whispers and nudges as we gawked at his colourful tattoos. He was hardcore covered front and back, right to left to goodness knows where, and down to his elbows.

This 'Marks' back job brought to life a sea-scene dominated by a large squid-like creature with a phallic head. Obscene. Tentacles laced with hungry suction cups groped around his sides. A tall ship sailed rough blue waves with white caps. Demons leered. Skulls grinned. Barbed wire and Japanese art finished the edges. They hinted of stories you'd rather not hear. Art imitated life. His moko. Well, now he had my attention, or morbid fascination. I glared at him as he buttoned up his shirt. Meg was smiling. I rolled my eyes, blew smoke into his face and shook my head. No comment.

"Having a good birthday, Meg?" I asked.

"Yea, not bad. I'm working, but I love my job. The folks called from Maungaturoto this morning. That was nice," she said. "Funny how we both come from up north but didn't meet until we came to the big smoke, hey?"

"Totally, mate. So nuts."

Meg still had her sweet, natural quality. I liked that about her. Time sure went slowly when you weren't drinking. I was bored. The happy hour crowd drifted in and people huddled in their natural cliques. Meg chatted happily to her customers. My thoughts turned to the new fabric I'd bought for a black suit. I'll slide off soon, I decided, and get sewing. Once I saw an outfit in my mind, I couldn't let it go until it was finished.

"So you're not drinking?" Mark asked.

"No."

"Do you work around here?" he asked.

"Yep."

Inane questions kept coming, drawing monosyllabic responses. My dislike grew.

"Wanna come out for a smoke?" Mark asked.

Bingo! I was keen for that. Finally, he'd said something interesting. I was stinging to get stoned. I didn't want to take his smoke though. He'd think I owed him.

"I'll get mine from my car."

I reached under my seat where I'd cunningly stashed it. Icy turquoise eyes followed me.

"What the f*@k are you doing stashing your gear under there? That's the first place the pigs look!" he said. "And how much did you pay for this crap? It's rubbish." He had a talent for making someone feel like both a complete dumbass, and as angry as hell at the same time.

"F*@k off, asshole. You're just a spoilt rich kid," I said. "I hate spoilt rich kids."

He reminded me of the spoilt kid in Shrek Ever After who kept saying, "Do the roar." I could hardly see past his over-inflated sense of entitlement. He was a sick boy. We had a smoke and went back to the pub.

"We're off now. We're pub-crawling for my mate's stag night."

"Bye."

'Good riddance,' I thought.

"He's a really nice guy," Meg said, watching him leave with the boys. "I've known Mark for years."

"Really?" I said, wondering if we were talking about the same person. I'd never met anyone so disagreeable. He was as subtle as a sledgehammer. We were a lot alike.

At work the next day, I'd already put the unpleasant individual out of my mind. Typing up an urgent report for one of the financial analysts, my fingers flew. The pressure was on. Life in the Group Account Executive (GAE) team mirrored my own. It was all or nothing.

I blocked out the person standing at my desk until she spoke. "Hey Janet, there's someone in the foyer to see you," Gilda said.

"Who is it?" I huffed. I wasn't expecting anyone.

"I don't know. He wouldn't say."

"Ok, thanks Gilda."

I saw him through the glass as I let myself through the security doors on the twenty-third floor. Sigh. How did he even know where I worked?

"Gid'ay," the tooth diamond flashed, winningly.

"What do you want?" I demanded.

"I wanted to say hello," he said. A little off-guard, he feigned confidence.

"Hello," I said. "Goodbye."

Turning on my heels, I disappeared back through the security doors. I sat back down at my desk. My heart was thumping. I tried to pick up where I left off. I was single for a reason.

"How's the report going, Janet? Nearly there?" It must really be urgent for Peter to ask.

"Yep, nearly there Pete," I said, trying to regain my composure.

How did he know where I worked? Meg!" The state of her! This was a breach of the castle walls. The next day at work the phone rang.

"Hello, Janet speaking."

"Gid'ay," Mark said.

"Eh?"

"Do you want to come to lunch?" he asked.

"Ah, no. I don't." I hung up.

How did he get my number? Meg, f*@k! What was she thinking?

Every day Mark rang and asked me out for lunch. 'Well, if he thinks he's stubborn, I'll show him stubborn,' I thought. Every day for two weeks I said no. But he wasn't going away until I went to lunch with him. I caved. He won.

"Gid'ay," he grinned as I got into the black BMW.

"Hi."

He drove. Fast. Heavy gold rings gleamed in the sun. Awkward.

We snorted a couple of lines for lunch and smoked a stinky joint for dessert. Back at work, off my face, I was ten foot tall, bulletproof and crystal clear. Or so I thought. I was hooked. The next day was the same, and the day after that. Then there was no looking back. He was really interesting when he wasn't obnoxious. We had much to talk about.

Slowly I grew to love and depend on Mark. But I was starting to wonder why I was seeing him only during lunch hours. He told me nothing. He was an enigma. I had a question. His shirts were always perfectly ironed. He wasn't the ironing type. I had to see him on his terms. I was never allowed to see where he lived. We pulled up outside work. Lunch hours literally sped by these days. The question erupted out of the blue.

"I'm single. Are you?"

"No. I have a wife, a kid, and one on the way."

I felt like I'd been given the bash. Winded. Gobsmacked. Now I was a marriage wrecker. The 'other woman.' My head spun. I felt ill.

"I'd never have gone out with you if I'd known you were married."

"I know."

Numb, I hauled myself out of the car and back to work. Gilda saw my face. She had studied me carefully when I returned from lunch lately. She was a good friend. We covered for each other.

"Janet, are you ok?"

"He's married!" I wailed and trumpeted into a tissue. Gilda discretely ushered me off to a quiet room. Inconsolable, I wept until I was sick to my stomach. My heart broke. There was no more work that day. When the crying storm subsided, another layer of concrete hardened over my heart, insulating me against reality that little bit more. I loved him.

෴෨෭ ෨෭෴

Decision time. I wanted to do the right thing. To never see him again. But things had changed. I had changed. I was too weak, and addicted. Painful weeks went by, painful for everyone. The rumour mill turned. Emotions churned. Guilt. Anger. Self-contempt. Jealousy. Shame.

"Hi," Mark said as he opened the car door for me.

"Hi."

"How are you?" he asked, pulling out quickly into the traffic.

"Ok," I said, taking the joint.

"My missus knows."

"What did she say?"

"She'd fight for me. Someone told her you always go for married men."

Wow. There it was again. The blindside. "What the f*@k! I've never gone out with a married man in my life! Ask Meg!" Oh yep, who was going to believe that, now I was the antagonist in my own story.

"What do you think?" I asked Mark.

Silence.

"I don't know."

He wasn't going to ask Meg because he wanted to believe I did go for married men. Was he playing me? Had he forgotten he was the one who had stalked me? Valid questions, but in shock I was incapable of a cognitive process. Confusion reigned and I just couldn't seem to reconcile my thoughts and feelings with the facts, never mind put them into a cohesive sentence. My heart compass moved a few degrees south. Colder.

So began the subtle twisting of situations. An insidious tool which was to erode my self-confidence and grip on the truth.

⁂

Ten weeks after the accident, Marlene was discharged from hospital to continue her convalescence at her parents home. The wide-open plains of her world had shrunk to the size of a small yard. Her marital life had been dismantled and was now no more than a stack of boxes, memories and a bleeding heart.

The road to recovery was both rugged and long, but even the longest journey begins with just one step. Marlene's courage made sure she travelled that road, at times, inch by inch, one forward, one back.

But travel it she did.

Our paths weren't to cross again for many years. Both families travelled their own roads at their own speed in their own ways. Marlene's life was far from over. It had just taken a different turn. It took her alongside a river she had cried, which in time dried up. It took her down an old road where she would meet up with her new husband. Against the odds, in time, her world expanded to include four amazing children. Her heart blossomed and flourished with love and laughter.

But years crept by beneath the purple pines,
and veiled the Scar with grass and moss once more,
and left it fairer now with flowers and vines
than it had been before.

There was a wound once in a gentle heart,
from which life's sweetness seemed to ebb and die;
and love's confiding changed to bitter smart,
while slow, sad years went by.

Yet as they passed, unseen an angel stole and laid a
balm of healing on the pain, till love grew purer in the
heart made whole, and peace came back again.

Streams in the Desert, June 22

తితిత

"I've been kicked out," Mark said. The short statement hid a world of
pain in the hearts of a family. Bombshell.

"Well, you can stay with me." I was beginning to think it was my fault.
After all, everything always was. I was a bad person. If someone wanted to
love me, why would I send him away? However, it wasn't long before the
honeymoon was over. Mark's guilt and pain sought an outlet and I was a
moving target. I took so much to appease my own guilt, but my quota was
met pretty quickly.

"You need to go back to your family. You love them too much. This is
not working. Give it a hundred per cent to make it work because I won't
be here for you anymore," I said, bracing myself for an argument. Bracing
myself against the wall of pain I was about to hit.

"Ok."

He knew it was true. I almost fell over when the resistance I'd expected
didn't come.

"Please don't call in or ring me. I need space to get over you."

"Ok."

The door closed behind him. A monsoon of grief poured down on top
of me and overflowed out of my face and ran off my chin. He was larger
than life. And he wasn't here anymore. Emptiness had become tangible
matter. The place was thick with it. The silence deafening. There's just no
way around some things. Heartache is like that. You can deny and postpone
its onset with busyness, work or people, shopping, drink or drugs, but
eventually you have to front up and muscle through it.

Free to chain-smoke, I smoked myself sick. Cigarettes smouldered in
the ashtray as I threw myself into a new sewing project. I needed to put
some space in between the past and the present, while I created a new
reality. Pain seemed to cause time to stop, but gradually days and weeks and
months ticked over. Mark gave me time and space in the beginning, really

giving it a proper go back at home.

But it wasn't to last and he began ringing up.

"Hello?"

"Hi." Silence. "Stop ringing. I told you. I'm moving on."

"Can I come over?"

"No. Bye." Click.

The phone rang again, grating my nerves. It wasn't easy to be strong all the time, but I was trying. I had set my face like flint and my heart on moving forward — on my own. This time I was single and was going to stay single.

"Hello?"

"Hi, it's Stefan. How are you?"

He was just a friend. I knew he liked me, but he wasn't my type. He persevered with our friendship in the hope his patience would be rewarded. I liked talking with him about spirituality, altered states and occult crap. I was extremely intrigued by the supernatural, about which he seemed to know. After all, he was a hypnotist: it was his job. I had visited his office a few times. He'd attempted to hypnotise me in the 'pod'. It never really worked, just frustrated me.

"Some people are just too strong to be hypnotised," he had said.

"Ok."

"Do you want to do a photo shoot at Mount Eden Railway Station tomorrow? It's going to be a good day for it." I looked out at the overcast sky. Patches of blue peeked through the holes in the soft grey blanket.

"Yea, all right. Pick me up about ten o'clock. I'll get some outfits together to bring."

Stefan had some new camera gear he wanted to check out, and it was as good an excuse as any. I started going through the outfits I would take. The tight white fishtail skirt with long chiffon gathers on the bottom would be a winner. I had fun gathering a few of my favourite pieces. My emotions were all over the show. The idea of being in a photo shoot was good for my self-esteem; however, I hated having my photo taken. Every photo of myself I'd seen so far was nasty.

Early the next morning the phone rang. For goodness sake, what freak was ringing in the middle of the night?

"What?"

"Can I come over?" Mark asked.

"NO. And stop ringing!" had become the standard script.

The phone was becoming an instrument of torture.

"I don't want to do it without you. I want to leave for good," he said. The BMW motor hummed in the background. My heart weakened. I sighed, leaning back on my pillows.

"Ok," I said, glancing at the clock. 6 a.m. "But you'd better be sure. And don't take your guilt out on me because I'm not taking any more of your crap."

I stood on the edge of the darkest decade, like Frodo looking over the dead marshes knowing he had to find a way to cross. Eleven years later, when the thrill of new adventure had long since passed, I would summon the strength to raise my hand through the suffocating muck for help.

If we could know beyond today as God does know,
Why dearest treasures pass away,
And tears must flow;
And why the darkness leads to light,
Why dreary paths will soon grow bright;
Some day life's wrongs will be made right,
Faith tells us so.

Streams in the Desert, July 29

3. The makeover

1991

The stripping of my manufactured identity began with the visible layers first. Mark and I were finding that our jobs had become a serious handbrake on our lifestyle, so we both quit. We were outlaws going wherever the Harley took us, living off drug money and mates. Somewhere in there my world view had undergone a major modification. The general population was now a grey army of drones chasing the New Zealand Dream: house, beach house, 2.5 kids and a dog. Drones without backbone or spirit, wasting their lives behind a desk or wheel working for the man to fund their appetite for more, more, more.

"I'm going to move a couple of loads tonight. Can you come with me?" I asked Mark.

I was moving out of my Mount Albert flat bit by bit while I had time. I saw no purpose in keeping the flat when I was never there. Having a home didn't seem to matter anymore. Mark and I crashed wherever these days, mostly at Dave and Sues. Mark was staying in a little room off Dave and Sue's garage. My beautiful sister, Sam, let me store my stuff at her flat. She didn't like Mark, or the change in me. She wasn't one for talk. Her blue-grey eyes said it all.

"No, I can't tonight. There's something I have to do," he answered with the usual obscurity.

"I've got a bad feeling. Like something's going to happen. I can't explain it."

Automatically, Mark reached into the driver's door side-pocket and passed me the Beretta. "It's fully loaded. The safety's on. Take it, just in case." I dropped the piece into my trench-coat pocket.

"Thanks," I said, smiling. Beretta was the Rolls Royce of handguns. It was small, but it demanded respect. Less was definitely more. I drove to the flat with foreboding riding shotgun. Going about my business behind closed curtains, I packed my things for an hour or so. The flat had a cold, desolate atmosphere. Dead midges and bugs had accumulated on the unkempt floors. The stressed-out plants were being eaten alive by parasites. One flat-mate had moved out hastily after I'd confronted her about using all my skincare products. The solitary Asian student had always fended for himself, surfacing only for food and now he too had gone.

I didn't like being here anymore. It was like stepping back into the parallel drone universe from which I had evolved. I was glad to be leaving. I never had been a great planner or goal-setter, but now I didn't like thinking further ahead than the next five minutes. Blindness and denial had stolen my vision, imprisoning me in the present moment. All regard for consequences, other people's feelings and concerns and even the concept of right and wrong was discarded on the floor of my old flat, shed like an old skin.

It hadn't been the same after the break-in a couple of weeks ago. I'd found my bedroom window broken. Leaves and spiders decorated the carpet amidst the broken glass. It had obviously been a few days. A shudder wracked me. The violation of my personal space was another reason that when I was here I felt like a visitor in someone else's house. Only one thing had been taken. A brand new ounce of cannabis had been hidden under some fabric on my sewing table. Someone had been watching. They knew it was there. Double yuck. So was the feeling they were coming back. The curtains did nothing to alleviate the feeling of being watched.

Shaking off uneasiness, I picked up a couple of boxes and heaved a weary sigh. Walking along the path behind the garage, I came face to face with a lowlife wedged into the corner. He was waiting for me. I was ready. I dropped the boxes, pulled the piece and flicked the safety off in one move. His eyes bugged in disbelief and he gapped it. I chased him down the shared drive wielding the firearm, ready to shoot his knees out. I didn't want to kill him, only to stop him, but he had disappeared into thin air. That was frustrating. I tossed the boxes into the car and punished the engine of my little red Anglia, keen to get away from this sad hole. That explained the premonition. I liked the power the gun had given me. I knew how to manage my anger. Pay it forward.

ༀ⊙ ⊙ༀ

"Let's get you some decent clothes," Mark said one day. The irony in that statement was lost on him. He took me to visit a friend, Muz. His friend dragged hard on her cigarette and watched with the eyes of a predator from nearby. She'd once been stunning, but tweaking had left her ravaged and scarred, inside and out. No style points there, but I failed to see that we were travelling the same road.

Mark tossed down a pile of soft nappa leather and barked at Muz. "Make her pants, a skirt and a top." He cut a couple of lines to get him going. Muz was away. The talented designer and upholsterer specialised in leather. His addictions were well on the way to ruining him and he, like so many others, would do anything for drugs. In a blur, he'd already re-upholstered the inside of Mark's BMW in black leather.

I stood still while Muz focused intently on gluing bits of leather onto me. Cutting the garments off me with strategic cuts, he sewed in the zips. There were pickin' pox on his face and arms; holes, scabs and scars where he'd picked and cut himself with a razorblade, digging for the scabies he felt burrowing beneath his skin. No one ever really knew whether or not they were real. I liked to think they were. His friend had cut herself a fresh nostril mining for hers.

Hours later, after whipping himself into a lather, Muz was done. If the new leathers weren't body paint, they'd do till we got some. Mark went the extra mile and bought skull earrings, drilled holes through them and threaded them onto the laces in the front of the camisole. A gold skull ring with ruby eyes finished my trash look. Mark was my self-appointed stylist. In the beginning I cringed at the things he bought or had made for me to wear, and wondered whether he could be serious. But it wasn't long before I no longer minded wearing them, but had also learned to ignore the stares of even hardened-edition Westies.

I'd always taken such care with my clothes, spending hours, months and years of my life crafting handmade, original pieces. My wardrobe was full of exquisitely tailored and lined suits, jackets, skirts and tops. Anything I wanted, I made. I'd spent a large chunk of my childhood learning dressmaking from an authentic, card-carrying domestic goddess. Mum. If I wasn't sewing, I was hand-washing or ironing. This, however, was a different dimension and that was a different person. My devolution was almost complete, from corporate girl to skank.

Still, there were parts of me that were naïve and vulnerable. There were a few times in the early days with Mark when I freaked out. I didn't know Mark very well and had taken his hand and very quickly entered a different culture with him. Many of his mates were tattooed to the max. This was different for starters. Some sat around blasting drugs up their arms, and spending hours cleaning their guns and Harleys. So was that. In the beginning we'd been civilised and snorted the stuff, but the facade soon fell and we just got down to what Mark had been doing for years; blasting it. Especially that.

It was my job to sit around looking hot or whatever, trying to figure out who everyone was and what was really going on. This got old quite quickly. I denied how bored I was and told myself I should feel honoured to be chosen. I was deeply shocked at the needles, and in fact had needle-phobia from way back. When I had my first blast, I was really freaking. It occurred to me (after the fact) that Mark could have easily injected me with anything at all, used a dirty needle, or given me way too much. My phobia was to pull a U-turn and become addiction. Needle addiction.

◈◈◈

One afternoon at Dave's, I was cooking steaks; our first feed in a week. This was scary enough, as I didn't know how to cook steak well. We'd been on meth all week, and we were wrecked. We'd had no sleep for five days and nights, very little or no food, and not much to drink. Dave and Mark were at the table cleaning their guns. Drug paraphernalia was scattered amongst the weaponry on the table. We were all off our faces, as usual.

The bullet hole in the stainless steel bench spoke of the day Dave's handgun accidentally fired when he was cleaning it. He hadn't realised there was a bullet in the chamber. The bullet whistled past Mark's ear as he was heading for the door, ricocheted around the kitchen and somehow missed Dave. Staring vacantly at Mark and Dave I held the pan in one hand, tipping the frying pan from side to side to make to the juices run to the dry parts. When had the paradigm shift happened? When had all this become normal? When had all this become ok? It had all happened so fast, my mind hadn't processed the massive life-change yet. My body wasn't used to the pure drugs. I had the speed wobbles. Literally. It was just as well heroin hadn't agreed with me.

Then it happened. Almost audibly the psychotic switch flicked in my head. I wigged out. Mark and Dave suddenly looked like people I should be very scared of. A book that had horrified me as a kid flashed in my memory. It was called 'My Friends Are Dying'. The cover shot showed a heavily tattooed guy sitting at a blue Formica table with a tourniquet around his arm, shooting up. The tattoos had shocked me. The needle and drugs had shocked me. Even the hideous blue Formica table had shocked me. And now, here I was in Dave's kitchen, a snapshot of that very picture, minus the blue Formica, but somehow worse. Worse, because it wasn't someone else, it was me.

Everything they were saying about the plan they were making to kill me made perfect sense. Or so I thought. This was Drug Induced Psychosis 101, but it was no hypothetical study. They were calmly discussing how they were going to kill me as I cooked their dinner. I imagined rubber sheets rolling out and my blood spilling as they filmed their evil movie.

My mind was losing traction and breathing became convulsive gasps. I tried and failed to come to terms with the dramatic pendulum swing from needle-phobic to needle maniac overnight. Everything seemed so hard core. I couldn't cope. My life now depended on whether they were nice people underneath it all, or not. It depended on luck.

The phone rang, Dave answered. He calmly continued discussing my imaginary movie production with the caller. It all made perfect sense. Oh no, my parents. They were in on it too. They'd raised me just for this purpose, to die in this sick movie. They'd always known. Why did mum bother teaching me sewing? My sister was in on it too. So were all my friends. An emotional tsunami threatened my consciousness. Betrayal, grief, and fear.

Of course it was true. They looked like hell. They were certainly capable. It was just another day at the office for them. All strength left my fingers. Shock ruled. The sizzling fry pan clanged harshly to the floor; steaks splattered. The guys jumped.

"What the f*@k? Those steaks cost me my last ten bucks!" shouted Dave.

I backed towards the door not taking my eyes off them for a second. I was out the door, backing up the driveway. I couldn't turn my back to them. They weren't getting anywhere near me; I would make sure of that. By the time Mark came to his senses I was already at the gate. I fled.

"Hey wait up. What's the matter? Stop!" he bellowed.

I was the fastest woman on earth at that moment and wasn't about stop and have a chat. Knowing he'd have to punch me out cold to stop me, Mark instituted Plan B. Pursuit. I wildly wondered whether it really was the day I thought it was. Maybe I'd actually lost days or weeks and hadn't even known. I burst into the nearest dairy huffing and puffing, Mark chasing up close behind. The shopkeeper was serving someone, but this was a matter of life and death. Eyes wild and nostrils flaring, I begged, "Please, I have to use the phone." I checked the newspaper date. Cool. Ok, so I hadn't lost days. Whew.

"No I'm sorry, you cannot be using the telephone please."

I ran. There was no one to ring anyway. Everyone I knew was in on it. Every house on every street that whizzed passed me was in on it. My imagination had created film sets in every house ready and waiting just in case I chose that house to run into. Each car that passed was cruising to do a drive-by. The world was in on it.

Mark gave up the chase and dragged his butt back to Dave's place.

"PACK EVERYTHING UP! SHE'S FLIPPED! Call G and get him over here. He can dump everything. The cops will be here any minute."

They didn't really know me either, so prepared for the worst. That I'd go to the cops and nark. They misunderstood me as badly as I'd misunderstood them. While Dave called G, Mark moved quickly filling a couple of plastic rubbish bags with the bare-essentials. Guns and drugs mostly. G arrived.

"Open your boot!" Mark demanded.

"What?"

Mark pushed him out of the way, dumped the bags in his boot and slammed it shut.

"Now dump it! Go!"

G is like, "What the f*@k?"

Mark lunged at him. G knew it was time to move. He jumped in his car and roared up the road. G was freaking. He felt as though every eye in the neighbourhood was on him; X-ray eyes that could see through the boot and into the bags, and even knew his name. Heck, they could probably smell it too. The dope was reeking. He couldn't think of anywhere to dump it in broad daylight. After driving around the block a couple of times, he took it back to Dave's, dumped it there again, and took off.

∾ର ଉର∾

I didn't stop until I found a place to hide. A little group of trees in a vacant lot between two houses looked safe. No people. That had to be good. I tried to morph into some trees so I'd be invisible from the road, although all I really had to do was turn sideways.

"Hi," came a voice from the side. I practically jumped out of my skin.

"What, and who the f*@k?" I thought, glaring at the old man. The old digger leant against his fence and looked at me.

"Are you ok?" he asked. I held his gaze, backing away. He was in on it. He knew.

"I can get my wife, she can help you."

He was still in on it. He still knew.

"You can come in and use the phone if you want to call someone."

"Ok," I squeaked. But he was still in on it.

Inside, I backed straight into the first corner so they couldn't sneak up on me. I didn't speak. He bought a stool so I could sit down.

"This is Mabel. I'm Vern."

They sat in their easy chairs and pretended to be normal. We stared at each other for a long time.

"What happened, dear?" asked Mabel kindly. "Did someone hurt you?" The clock ticked loudly. "Can you talk?" The thermostat clicked and the fridge shuddered.

"Would you like a cup of tea?" Oh yea, that'll fix it. You'll probably poison it anyway.

"Here's the phone, you can ring your friend," said Vern.

One by one, I went through everyone I knew. I sadly realised they were all in on it. There was no one to call. Surely there must be someone. Gilda, my friend from the bank. Yes, Gilda! Oh, no. I didn't have her number. F*@k! Vern brought a phone book. He was probably used to dealing with psychotics, living in West Auckland. With one eye on the olds, I scanned the pages. They weren't going to trick me. The internal dialogue went like this: "Where is it, is she in here? No, she's not in the phone book! That's it then, I'm done. Oh, yes she is, here she is. Is she home? I bet she's out, she goes out all the time!"

"Hello?" said Gilda. Relief is too mild a word.

"Gilda, can you come and get me? NOW? I'm in trouble."

"Yes of course. Where are you?" Damn, I had to talk to the olds.

"Roberts Road, Te Atatu. Watch your back. They'll be following you."

"Ok," she said, "I'll be there soon. Stay where you are."

I hung up and glared at Mabel and Vern. It wasn't over yet. I still had to get out of here.

Gilda arrived. I ran out, grabbed her hand and dragged her to the car. Leaping in, I whammed the seat down dead flat and stared at the ceiling.

"Drive!"

"Okay," she said, looking at me sideways. "We'll be home soon."

"Watch your rear-vision mirror. They'll be following us."

"Ok. I will."

Every bump on the road to Gilda's North Shore sanctuary jolted me further into the bowels of hell. Physically safe, even though I always was, I remained in great psychological peril. My life was a conspiracy. Grief was crushing me. My heart was aching under the pressure. Desolation stretched into the future, broken only by scenes of electric shock treatment, big injections, bouncy walls, straightjackets and echoing screams.

Again, I didn't know why I was fighting so hard to stay alive. Why? I had no family, only one friend; and I couldn't work ever again because everyone was in on it. The world waited their turn to kill me. Well, get in line! I could only die once.

"Are you watching?" I asked Gilda, annoyed at how relaxed she was. Man, she really needed to get with the programme.

I fell silent and stared at the ceiling. Gilda didn't answer. She was shocked at my gaunt face, wild eyes, scrawny body and (completely) mental state. Like Frodo, I had gone where no man could follow. She put me to bed. I slipped further into the abyss. I'd surely be melted by magma if I went any lower. Scenarios of being discovered at Gilda's played out. I felt a bit bad about putting Gilda's life in danger but I couldn't help that. Sorry.

A glimmer of hope flashed during the rare moments I came back to myself. Hope that after a good sleep I'd awaken to find it had all been just a nightmare. But then I tweaked out again, reliving the betrayal from every person I'd ever known, for hours. After a fitful night of waking and sleeping nightmares I discovered day was dawning. This was it. I was supposed to be 'normal' now. My right mind was supposed to have returned to pick up the pieces. But it hadn't. I was still out there somewhere. Dry throat clicked. Knuckles whitened.

This must surely be hell. I could sense demonic vultures circling, waiting for the twitching to stop. They perched on my shoulders and whispered in my ears. I was grateful they weren't pecking my eyes out. Yet. I was powerless to stand against them. How does one lay hold of the unseen? Gilda, where are you? Why aren't you coming to check on me? Why aren't I ok now?

Miserably marshalling my waning strength I dragged myself to the toilet. The calendar on the toilet door was IN ON IT! It fitted perfectly. How could I keep getting worse, when I had stopped taking the drugs? Had I moved into withdrawal? I seriously doubted my ability to come back now. This was worse than insanity because I knew it. Insane people don't know they're mad, do they? I was completely unhinged and flapping in the wind.

In the sporadic moments approaching clarity, I held onto the glimmer of hope for tomorrow. That maybe tomorrow, after a good night's sleep, my faculties would return.

Unfortunately, the 'good night's sleep' was once again a slippery foe I couldn't catch. Instead, I waded waist deep through delirium until the merciful sunrise pried dark fingers off the city.

This was it. I steeled myself for the big reveal. I would do my mental checks and would find 'I' had returned. But I hadn't. I was the same. Psychotic. Paranoid. Mortally depressed.

Everything was still the same! How could everything still be the same? Someone call the vet and get this over with!

Or someone may be chastened on a bed of pain with constant distress in their bones, so that their body finds food repulsive and their soul loathes the choicest meal. Their flesh wastes away to nothing, and their bones, once hidden, now stick out. They draw near to the pit, and their life to the messengers of death. *Job 33:19–22*

Drone army: 1, Outlaws: Nil. The drone existence was looking pretty good to me right about now.

"That's it," I decided, relaxing my grip on hope and watching it drift away on the black current. It's over. No one I knew had been 'gone' that long. Not even the real spinners! I began to come to terms with the reality of enduring the rest of my days and sleepless nights rocking backwards and forwards as the world carried on selfishly with their lives.

ᕫᕫ ᕫᕫ

"Janet?" Gilda's brown eyes peered through the crack in the door. "Oh, good, you're awake. Would you like to join me for a cup of tea and some toast?"

She was a champion, pretending not to notice the wild leathers, matted hair, pickin' pox and horribly skinny legs sporting goose bumps and tree-stumps. I'd changed a lot since she'd seen me last. The girl with the sparkle who'd worked at the bank, was no longer. She spoke gently in loving tones. Speech was still cowering behind a tree somewhere, peering at me and whispering behind its hand. Speech was for winners. I listened from somewhere out there to Gilda's conversation; her comforting noises. Like everything was going to be all right.

"I had planned to fly to Wellington this weekend. It was strange. My client rang and cancelled the meeting at the last minute. I didn't end up going. I'm glad I didn't, now."

So was I. Where would I be now, if she had? The morning sun warmed my legs and the tea warmed my heart and soul. There was a knock at the door. Gilda looked at me. My heart raced. Gilda opened the door. I heard Mark's voice. Was this real?

"Is Janet here?"

"Yes, she is," said Gilda, opening the door to let him in.

Mark looked rudely out of place in the older woman's peaceful sunroom. Black leather and tattooed flesh rudely confronted floral fabric and frilly cushions. I saw relief on his face, which I mistook for love. I felt codependency, which I mistook for love. I realised I missed him. I couldn't stay away even if I wanted to.

Something weird happened. My two worlds collided. The impact blew the psychosis away. I had something real to grasp onto again. I welcomed new action to replace the show-reel of horror that had played on a loop. I found a voice and thanked Gilda with it then jumped on the bike behind Mark to carry on where we had left off.

Gilda stared as the hog went through its gears, rupturing the peace of the sleepy neighbourhood.

"What would it take to snap someone out of living like that? I would hate to think," Gilda thought as she closed the door.

Yet if there is an angel at their side, a messenger, one out of a thousand, sent to tell them how to be upright, and he is gracious to that person and says to God, 'Spare them from going down to the pit; I have found a ransom for them — let their flesh be renewed like a child's; let them be restored as in the days of their youth' — then that person can pray to God and find favour with him, they will see God's face and shout for joy; he will restore them to full well-being. *Job 33:23-26*

---

4. The visitor

1994

Mark plonked me in my deconstructed room and appointed Muz's girlfriend as my caregiver. The wild and gorgeous blonde was dressed, of course, in custom-Muz leathers with Guns 'N Roses flair. We went shopping for soup stuff. I trudged around Foodtown in Grey Lynn after Stana like a mannequin. My adrenal gland was on holiday owing to overwork and every enzyme and hormone in my body had gone looking for it. From time to time Stana held up various vegetables for me to inspect. I looked at them blankly, unable to pull a facial, or externalise my agony. Who cares about f*@kin carrots? My cigarette money was wasted on food, thank you very much.

Stana prepared the soup and told me it was going to be ok. But I knew it wasn't. Everything in my life was very, very wrong. I was cloaked in a black feeling I couldn't shake or explain, even to myself. My life was a fricking nightmare. A joke. A lie. A major drag. My life? Who was I anyway? Who was this soulless, miserable creature who stared back at me from the mirror? What was it all for? Was there a point? What was the meaning of life? Is Monty Python the only other person who cares about that? You can't get a serious answer out of him! The desire for an answer to this question seemed to niggle more and more every day.

The three-day psychotic episode was one thing, but intermittent psychosis toyed with me persistently like a cat with a mouse. It wasn't allowed to kill me, but it loved to watch me twitch. A door had been opened and it wasn't quite shut. Subconsciously I knew I had to pick up my life and never think about Mark again. I'd see whether the landlord would let me keep my flat after all. Surely Mark would never want to see me again after that performance anyway. What a tweaker. I was disgusted with myself. Embarrassed. Ashamed. Even though he'd looked for me until he found me, I swung wildly between the polar opposites of self-condemnation and questioning his agenda.

The phone rang. It was Mark.

"What are you doing?"

"What? What the freaking hell do you think I'm doing?" I shouted. "Recovering, or trying to. I don't know if I ever will yet!"

"I'm moving into the studio," Mark said as if I hadn't said anything. "You can come and stay with me there."

Phill Matthias had founded Dermagraphic Tattoo Studio in Ponsonby in the 1980s, and built a business that thrived for the next two decades. When Phill asked Mark to live out the back of the shop for security, I doubted whether he had intended Mark bring his baggage with him, but Mark was a law unto himself. I should say goodbye to Mark, but I was stunned that he still wanted me. I was torn. He validated me. Low self-image and codependency were the winners on the day.

"Ok."

It was meant to be a short-term arrangement, but we overstayed two very long years. Hideous African masks were the welcoming committee. The scary faces lined both walls of the hallway in the old villa. Tattoo art covered the rest. This place had history that went way back.

And these walls could talk. The place was alive.

༺ ༒ ༒ ༻

Mark and I had been living at the tattoo studio a while when I got a call from Mum.

"I've arranged a photo shoot at the Russell Hamlet studio in Ponsonby

Road for you and Sam. I want to get some nice photos of you both before you turn to crap," she said, reflecting a somewhat disturbed mental process. My brother, Robert, had been photophobic and had turned avoiding the camera into an art form. Subsequently we were left with few photos of him.

"Ok thanks. I think."

"You can meet your sister up there at 2 p.m on Wednesday. Don't forget!"

Not only did she capture photos of her beautiful daughters, but secured the cover shot for a book that would be written two decades later entitled, Take a Walk on the Wild Side.

A while later Mark worked out the knots in my shoulders and the glorious warmth from the heater warmed us this freezing winter's night. It was 3 a.m, and again, we'd been on meth five or six days and nights non-stop. Again. It's fair to say we were in bad shape. Usual story: going a hundred miles an hour the whole time, very little food or drink (if any), and no sleep at all. Suddenly ice touched my back. But it was more than just cold. It was the biting cold of nitrous oxide. It was the filth of an evil spirit touching my skin and reaching for my soul. Fear that transcends any other fear slammed into me, head-on.

So what does one do when one can't be strong in the Lord and His mighty power because one doesn't want to know him? What does one do when one is standing before the enemy without the full armour of God, spiritually naked and utterly powerless? Well, I wouldn't recommend your finding out, but this is how I approached this particular challenge. I leapt a foot or more off the ground, punched my fist high in the air and roared, "I'm strong!" This would have been comical had it not been so serious. Strong I most certainly was not.

Then it hit me like a freight train through the top of my head. *Wham!* In that split second, a demon entered my body, forcing my own spirit straight out. It was the freakiest feeling. My useless words and emotions were as helpful as throwing a handful of flour into a tornado. Instantly, here I am watching this reality horror show from very high up — from far beyond the ceiling. This sounds impossible, but anyone who has experienced astral travel knows what I mean. I freaked. Was I was ever going to be reunited with my earth-suit, or had I done it good and proper this time? Waster!

One hundred kilometres further north in my hometown of Ruawai around 4 a.m this freezing night, our dear friend Mary was woken by God to pray. He knew whom to call on when he meant business.

"On your knees now, Mary. Pray for Jan!" he said.

"Oh Lord God, it's the middle of winter, can't I just pray in bed?"

"Out of bed! On your knees. Now!"

She moved quickly and prayed hard until the Spirit of God told her it was ok to stop.

The weapons we fight with are not the weapons of the world. On the contrary, they have divine power to demolish strongholds. *2 Corinthians 10:4*

The foul spirit left me and went straight into Mark. He gasped like he'd been winded and looked different instantly. His persona was that of someone else. His spirit was different. His mannerisms were different. There was a different 'person' in Mark's body. It was trippy. Mark's spirit had officially left the building but still seemed close by, although I couldn't see it. I heard his voice speak through his mouth, on occasion, when he was allowed, which wasn't often. He was now a guest.

As I had known, Mark also knew he was in deep shit. Then, as with me, randomly the thing retreated, and Mark was allowed back into his body, looking like himself again. Whew, that was lucky, I thought, unaware of the spiritual battle raging because of the prayers of a faithful friend. In our arrogance, I thought we'd overcome it ourselves. Joke. Had we imagined it? Was this Psychosis 102? We knew we were in a dodgy state, but the fact that it had happened to both of us took it to a whole new level. This was no psychosis: take it from an expert.

"We're in trouble! Call Stefan. Tell him to get here now!" Mark said.

Indeed. Let's get the opinion of a learned colleague. We both believed Stefan was our only hope, a hypnotist by trade, and the authority in spiritual matters, so we thought. I listened to the phone ring, willing Stefan to pick up.

"Huh?" Stefan croaked.

"Stefan, an evil spirit came into Mark. We need you, can you come now?"

"Don't do anything until I get there. I'm on my way."

"Ok. I won't do anything until you get here."

I put the phone down. Anger welled up inside me at the cheek of the thing. I didn't know that my own choices had given this darkness permission to invade my life. Ouija boards, drugs, séances, psychics, even horoscopes. Couple that with living in a haunted house, and staying up for a week frying my brain and you have a recipe for disaster. Nevertheless, I confronted it. I was clearly not going to use this particular point in time to start making wise choices. Like Aragorn and his army outside the gates of Mordor in the Lord of the Rings, I strode about the small apartment issuing a war cry to the foul thing.

"Come out and show yourself!" I demanded.

IMPORTANT NOTICE: Do not try this at home, peeps.

Unlike Aragorn, there was nothing valiant about this madness. Idiocy, insanity, indulgence; yes, but not valour. My bravado flowed from ignorance and arrogance. I paused in front of the kitchen sink. Suddenly a battalion of ants flowed out from a crack by the jug power point. They looked like a wide-angle shot of the army of Mordor, a unit moving together with a single purpose, a black plague. I blinked, not sure whether or not it was an hallucination. Before I could ask Mark whether he could see them they were sucked back into the crack, and were gone. And therein lay its response. I had my answer.

The Mouth of Sauron had asked Aragorn, who had the authority to have an audience with him, and to his surprise, Aragorn did. I, however, had neither authority nor army nor faculties. Woefully ill-prepared, I had in truth run onto the battlefield in my underwear. Gulp. I turned to tell Mark, but reeled back from the flies that filled the room. The air was thick with pestilence. Again, they flew in unity like a black squadron. Then, just as suddenly as they'd come, they too, vanished.

Mark let Stefan in.

"Ok, what's happened since we talked on the phone?" he asked, reading our shocked expressions.

Before we could speak, once again the thing hit Mark and once again, Mark wasn't Mark. Mark just didn't move like that. He didn't move his body like that, and he certainly didn't move his eyes like that. It glared at us. In creepy slow motion it took a seat at the table with its strange eyes glued on us. Stefan spoke to me without taking his eyes off it or even blinking.

"Don't say anything. Leave the talking to me. *And don't ask about the white light!*"

Just as Gandalf had warned Peregrin Took as they entered Lord Denethor's castle, like Pippin I was quick to agree, but failed to comply. No surprises there.

"Ok, I'll leave the talking to you," I said.

Stefan sat down at the table opposite 'Mark,' and studied it. I took a seat on the small couch in front of a wall mirror, facing the table. I reached for a pen and paper to take minutes, and waited obediently with pen poised. This was a good time to start being professional. I didn't want to miss anything. I was fascinated.

"What do you want?" Stefan asked.

"I came to visit Mark," said the demon, annoyed at the intrusion.

"Who are you?"

"Mark. My name is Mark," it said. It sat with its hands on its Mark's thighs, but they weren't resting on his thighs, they were a couple of inches above. It believed its legs were a lot bigger than Mark's legs actually were.

My Mark spoke from the corner through his body.

"It's my friend, Mark!" Pain loaded his voice. Love. Grief. The unspoken. "We were best friends. When we were sixteen we travelled around the world together. We came back when we were twenty. As soon as we got back he wanted to go again but I didn't want to. I stayed here and got married, and had my son. Mark went to live in Australia. He bought a farm and became a drug lord over there. It's him! My friend! Oh, I've missed you so much!"

"Are you sure it's him?" I asked my Mark.

It sighted me in its dirty gaze as if seeing me for the first time. Its lip curled back from its teeth in distaste. It hated me on sight. Stefan shot me that look; 'I told you not to say anything, remember.'

"Yea," my Mark managed to say before he had to retreat again.

Flies filled the room again, but I didn't flinch. I wouldn't break gaze with the thing. It wasn't going to see my fear. I wouldn't blink.

"There are flies on your c*%#," it hissed.

I didn't flinch. This was getting yucky. It hated that it couldn't get a reaction. It got mad. Stefan stepped in to provide covering fire.

"So you came to visit Mark," he said. It ignored the one who was asking what he'd already been told.

"I've missed you," it whined to Mark in a horrible pinched voice, and nearly started to cry. Suddenly it launched into telling a story. It was like we'd just turned the television on in the middle of a hard-core drama.

"When we were in Aussie working in the mines, we were in Perth and they were waiting for us to come out of the toilets and they were going to kill us as soon as we came out," it erupted like a boil being lanced.

My Mark spoke up, "Yea, you always got us into trouble and I always had to get us out. And you were twice the size of me, but you couldn't fight for shit!"

That explained the hands on the legs. Wow. 'Mark' must have been a big guy. My Mark wasn't small.

"A guy came in and warned us they were going to do it. He told us they were waiting out there for us and they were going to nail us as we came out," it bleated on.

Unmistakably my Mark again, "There was no way out of the toilets without them seeing us. So I took the tabs off a whole load of cans I found in the bin and put them on my fingers like rings, with the jagged bits at the top."

It said, "You went out swinging and peeled this guy's face right back to the bone." It's horrible voice dripped with bloodlust and pride.

Then my Mark, "They had to chopper him out. He would've died otherwise."

It said, "We had to leave Perth straight away after that and could never go back. They had it out for us man. That dude had been the man in Perth."

My Mark again, "We couldn't go back to our jobs. We had to leave Australia."

I was sickened by the story and the sound of its voice but wrote frantic notes, not wanting to miss anything. It sounded like a Freddie Kruger movie.

The stories poured out and it was hard to keep up. I wanted to pause and rewind. The conversation kept flicking back and forth between Mark and the thing, like two long lost buds that have missed out on a lifetime of news. Like they'd never had a chance to catch up and debrief after they came back from their world trip. They went from remembering one story, to the next, and onto the next one, then went back and picked up on earlier ones again. In the end they had about four stories going at once, flicking from one to the other. It was like channel surfing. All the stories were so real, like live-action sequences running simultaneously. When we moved onto the next one, I couldn't help wondering what was going on in the last one. I felt as though I was missing something.

They were both really excited; you could feel the strong connection and friendship. It was easy to tell them apart because of their voices, even though they were using the same mouth. Stefan was struggling. He was pale and had gone very quiet. My notes were getting fairly rough and rugged. I was leaning forward, totally engrossed, and before I realised what I was doing, I had said to it:

"Go back to the Russian cruise ship one, or the such-and-such one. You were just going to smash someone over the head with a rubbish bin when you skipped onto the next one."

It stopped, mid-sentence and fixed me with its terrible gaze. It had forgotten again that I was there. It slowly, subtly shook its head. It hated me more and more as time went on. Its eyes locked with mine and suddenly, in one fluid, unexpected motion it zoomed forward into my face until our noses almost touched.

"F*@k up, bitch," it hissed the words slowly. Its eyes stayed fixed on me as it recoiled in slow motion back to its chair.

Freaked out but not missing a beat I asked, "What about the white light?"

Stefan tasered me with a look. *Oops.* But I'd always been intrigued with the white light.

The visitor lost it.

It got up, savouring its hatred for me. Standing over me, it vomited a litany of foul names with cold, calculated malice that lifted the hair on the back of my neck. My poker face endured. Underneath, I was shaken but a deep-seated hatred of evil festered.

It answered, "If you want to know so bad, go and find out yourself, you f*@king bitch."

It despised me, but somehow it knew it couldn't cross the line into physical abuse, which made it angrier. Its weapons were intangible. Intimidation. Fear. Hate. Lies. It despised me because of Mary's prayer that had released the angels that tied its hands. It hated God and it hated the people made in his image. It hated me because I was receiving God's grace.

It hated that I didn't even know it, and certainly didn't deserve it. I was a sinner. But then that's what grace is. Unmerited favour. Jesus didn't come for the well — he came for the sick.

Frustrated, it sat down and blocked me out again, resuming an in-depth story about their part in the traditional line-crossing ceremony, when they had crossed the equator on the Russian cruise ship. Mark's body was beyond exhausted and badly dehydrated. He was in bad shape. I watched it still talking its head off and willed it to lift the glass of water I'd put in front of it and take a drink. It grabbed the glass and it lifted it slowly to its mouth, still talking. The glass almost got to its lips, then he put it down again, too engrossed in the story to drink. Then it suddenly stopped, and sat looking really sad and tired.

I wondered where my Mark was. Whether he'd ever be able to claim his body back and be rid of this hellish visitor. Whether he even wanted to. He was enjoying the visit a little too much for my liking. Would this be the end of Mark and me?

"It wasn't an accident," it said, out of the blue. "I was *murdered*."

"WHAT?" said Mark.

"It was a set-up. They made it look like an accident, but it was all planned!" it shouted with passion.

The awful accusation hung thickly in the air like a bad fart.

"Yea?" said Mark, interest kindled.

"I have a job for you to do. You've got to kill him for me" it said. "Make it right." The foul assignment to commit premeditated murder was straight from the bowels of hell. Something welled up inside me that I had thought long dead, buried and dried to dust.

"Wait up. No way! This is wrong. That just isn't going to happen," my voice growled.

A voice piped up that we hadn't heard for a while. Stefan.

"I'm out of here!"

That was the final straw for Stefan. He got up and left quickly. No one took any notice.

"You've got to! I was ripped off! I'm supposed to still be alive!" it lamented. *"Mark is the only one who can make it right! You have to do it. For me!"* it pleaded, convincingly playing the sympathy card.

What had happened so far was evil enough, but this was something else. I looked hard into its face. It had just overplayed its hand. Right there the occult lost its fascination for me, once and for all. All of a sudden it caught a glimpse of itself in the mirror behind me. It did a classic double-take and stopped dead. Slowly its head tilted on a slight angle and its brows creased as it tried to figure out what it was seeing. That wasn't the body it was expecting. Or maybe it was the angels it was seeing. God only knows, but it was caught right off-guard.

The prayer of a righteous person is powerful and effective. *James 5:16*

"That's right!" I took full advantage. "It's Mark's body, not yours!"

It looked at me, remembering once again why it hated me.

I carried on boldly winging it, thinking I was doing it all in my own strength. "It was nice of you to visit, but it is time to go now. You can come and visit another time, but for now it's over. Mark's tired. He needs a rest."

I hadn't known what was going to come out of my mouth — and I didn't mean that, but was willing to tell it anything to make it go. And I certainly didn't know what I was going to do next. I got up, grabbed it by the arm, and steered it down the hall to the front door. It allowed me to lead Mark's body like a meat puppet.

I opened the door and we stepped out onto the front veranda of the studio and into the weak sunrise. The creature of the night cringed against the light, weakened though it was. As the light hurts a vampire, it cringed and turned its head turned away from the east, away from the light of the world.

"Ok, bye," I said.

There was no dramatic sign, I wasn't totally sure it had left, but I had no option but to believe and hope it had. Mark's body was done. My Mark had returned, but was near collapse. The lights were on, but there was no one home.

"Hun?" I asked, hopefully peering into his face. "Let's go inside and get a drink of water."

I felt like things were never going to be the same again. Mark had mentioned his best friend once before. He'd told me they'd gone travelling around the world together, and that Mark had wanted to go again when they got back, but Mark hadn't. He'd never said any more than that. It had been too painful.

Mark skulled water. What could you say?

"One day when Mark was riding out front of his boys, a Mac truck hit him head–on. Peeled him out," Mark said. I was so relieved to hear Mark speaking properly through his own mouth. He looked so sad. "I've missed him so much. I've never told anyone. I've never spoken of the stories and things that happened overseas to anyone, ever," he said.

It was buried deep, but it was a fact.

All the stories they'd talked about were true. That was the first time since their travels they'd talked about their experiences together. Mark had been killed before they'd had a chance.

There we were at the end of a very long night, a very long night for us all. This is what it is to be saved by grace.

Many years later I came to understand that this visitor was not, in fact, Mark's friend Mark. It was a demon, a familiar spirit. Familiar spirits follow generational lines and know everything about a person or family. They are so convincing, because they have all the information there is to know.

The truth, is once a person has died they are no longer able to hang around the earth. It is only angels and demons that abide in the spiritual realm that sometimes overlaps our perception of reality.

Be strong in the Lord and in his mighty power. Put on the full armour of God, so that you can take your stand against the devil's schemes. For our struggle is not against flesh and blood, but against the rulers, against the authorities, against the powers of this dark world and against the spiritual forces of evil in the heavenly realms.
Ephesians 6:10-13

---

5.  S.O.S.

1996

Every ring of the phone assaulted my damaged nerves.

"Huh?" I grunted into the receiver. We'd only just dozed off after entertaining our hellish visitor.

"It's Stefan. I'm just ringing to say goodbye. I'm moving to Christchurch to look after my mother. She's sick."

"Oh, wow. I'm sorry, I didn't know she was sick." I didn't know because I didn't really care for other people's problems. But this all seemed very sudden.

"Thanks."

"When are you going?"

"Now. I've packed all my stuff into the car. I'm driving down."

What? I was having trouble processing. He was just leaving his business and everything? Walking away from his life just like that? He must have started packing the minute he got home from the studio last night.

"Oh wow." I said.

"Bye."

"Bye."

With that, he was gone, and that was the last time I ever spoke with Stefan. Mark was looking at me for an explanation.

"Stefan. He's moving to Christchurch. Right now." I said.

Mark's eyebrows rose. Laughter stirred in our bellies and couldn't be contained or controlled. We laughed and hysterically laughed. It felt good after the intensity of last night. The sound of a key wrestling with the lock on the front door made us stop and look at each other once again. Enter Tattoo Phill, artist and pioneer, the outlaw who changed the establishment from within. The legend.

"It's my birthday! We're versing the Auckland Bootgirls in war games out at Kumeu. You guys are on my team," Phill said to us. He waited for the joyous reaction to these glad tidings. When it didn't come, Phill went out to check the shop voicemail.

My heart dropped. My head had its own heartbeat. I felt like crap. Used up in every way, I didn't feel like games. Especially not running around the forest games playing stupid paintball.

"Oh, I don't wanna go," I said to Mark.

"Well, you have to," he said. "It's Phill's birthday."

"Yay!" I snarled. I was so unhappy.

When did I lose myself? Like a frog slowing boiling in water I hadn't noticed the water heating up little by little until it was too late, I was cooked. I'd tumbled down a few levels of Maslow's hierarchy of needs that was for sure. There was no doubt I was a bottom feeder with a long way to go before I realised my potential.

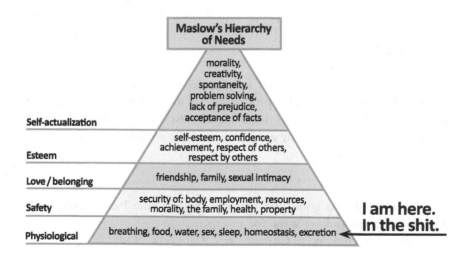

Ok, so I was at the bottom, and not even all my needs in that group were being met. Well, I still had a roof over my head for a few more minutes at any rate. With no breakfast and a pre–migraine headache, we set off to run around in the freezing rain. I was hangry (hungry and angry).

I loathe my very life; therefore I will give free rein to my complaint and speak out in the bitterness of my soul. *Job 10:1*

"You drive," Mark said. He wanted to sleep.

'Grrr,' my narrator growled miserably. Mark reclined in his seat and dozed.

Torrential rain fell in sheets. Condensation fogged the inside windows, just to cover all bases. Visibility was a thing of the past. I didn't know what 'driving to the conditions' was, so I didn't need to worry about that. It sounded like something old people did. I skimmed the lake in the fast lane until I just about floated into the car in front. Where the hell had that come from?

"F*@king idiots!" I screamed. The little car packed with big Pacific Islanders inched along in the fast lane. I took it personally. I'd put our lives at risk slamming on the pix just to avoid hitting them. The more I thought about it, the angrier I got. Then I realised they weren't even trying to get out of the way. They were still bouncing along as if they were the only ones on the road, enjoying themselves. That was it. I sped up until my bumper touched theirs. Then I floored it hard, ramming them forward. Their little car aqua-planed wildly. Heads whirled around, eyes bugged out in surprise. They gawked, incredulous, through the water streaming down the back windscreen. After the initial shock, they started laughing. I didn't. I rammed them again. This time they were shunted much further, dangerously out of control.

"Out of the fast lane, morons!" I shouted, giving them the Westie salute. Mark didn't open his eyes but shouted, *"Get out of her way!"*

I could see them shouting to the driver, leaning forward to make the car go faster. We were outnumbered, but that never mattered. What we lacked in numbers we made up for in fury. They floored it, but didn't have enough power to pass the car in the next lane. They had nowhere to go. Eventually, they willed their little bomb to pass and veered to safety, out of the line of fire. I sped past, spraying them with water, shouting expletives and shaking my fist in farewell.

Even as fools walk along the road, they lack sense and show everyone how stupid they are. *Ecclesiastes 10:3*

There's only one person this refers to here, and it's not the road rage victims.

I needed headache pills but didn't take unnecessary drugs. We found our team and geared up. I was the only girl in our team, and we were battling an entire team of girls. Never big on strategy, I took a hit from my team, in the butt, at point-blank range. This enhanced neither my demeanour nor my appreciation of the game.

Eventually, the infernal game in the stupid forest finished. We were then afforded the honour of being buried alive under a steaming heap of verbal excrement by the Bootgirls for allegedly cheating. Ok, for cheating. We probably cheated. I probably cheated without even knowing. Our duty was fulfilled; our friend's birthday celebrated, no thanks to me.

For there is a proper time and procedure for every matter, though a person may be weighed down by misery. *Ecclesiastes 8:6*

༜ཉྩ ঌ৯

The drive to Coromandel with Dave and Sue was also memorable for all the wrong reasons. I was in an ugly mood. Again. Obviously we'd run out of drugs, so that was a problem right there. For me, that is. Mark just got on with things when we ran out, but not me. Good cop, bad cop.

The atmosphere was rank. Mark and I were locked in mortal combat, trying to inflict as much damage on each other as possible with the fewest words, and not the most scintillating of travel companions. I was feral. Dave pulled up at KFC in Thames and turned the engine off with a heavy sigh, unable to take the punishment all the way to Coromandel without a break. Sue and I found a table as the guys foraged for food. My dull, sunken eyes tracked their every move. I needed to behave, so I could get some food into my sorry self. The smell of chicken and chips was torturous.

"They always have real fresh, tender chicken in Thames," Sue said to me, trying to placate the beast. All my focus went into keeping a lid on the volcanic hatred bubbling below the surface. The explosive negative energy of a P freak gone bad cannot be explained or contained for long. It will find an outlet, as our long-suffering, faithful friends well knew. Food finally arrived. Mark dropped the tray on the table.

"There you are, you sick f*@king bitch," Mark said. The final straw gently landed.

"Oh shit," Dave mumbled. Sue moved quickly.

It wasn't what he said. It was that he was right. I was a sick bitch. Automatically, I launched the steaming hot, juicy chicken breast into his face, point blank. Sue was right; it was fresh. So fresh it disintegrated all over Mark's forehead burning as only hot oil can. The split-second look of surprise was priceless. I couldn't help smiling.

Heaving my chair across the room, I bolted from the restaurant as if my life depended on it. I spun through the streets of Thames like a human tornado until I was sure I'd lost him. I sat puffing in my hiding place, once again, like the speed freak I was. I don't think I was enjoying everyday life, to be fair. Mark had wiped the burning fat and chicken particles off his forehead. The angry red patch fuelled his rampage through the restaurant. Diners nervously watched as he took the rest of the fried chicken and wiped the restaurant windows with it and screamed, "Look at what the bitch did to me!" This was one of Mark's personal favourite methods of self-expression. When the chicken wore out, Mark turned his attention to the tables and chairs. The proverbial bull in a china shop ploughed his way to the door, tables and chairs flying out each side as he exited the establishment.

Dave and Sue quickly and quietly joined him in the ute. Mark ordered them to drive on and leave me behind, but being the good friends they were, they combed the streets of Thames looking for me. Eventually, I allowed myself be found, and they talked me into rejoining the happy group. Dave and Sue aborted the Coromandel mission in favour of delivering their toxic load back to Auckland.

"You can sit on the back like the dog you are," Mark spat. "You're not sitting in the front with us."

"With pleasure," I replied, smiling at his glowing forehead. I sat on the back of the ute, freezing, famished and festering all the way back to Auckland. The lucky customers at the tattoo studio were privy to an encore performance upon our arrival until abruptly shut down by Phill's girlfriend.

I was an empty shell. I'd let my job and flat slip through my fingers. My car had been wrecked by a drunk-driver while it sat parked up out front of the studio. I missed my own space. I couldn't do the things I loved anymore. I was estranged from my family, and I had no girlfriends. No identity. I was an accessory, and not a very good one, now I was a complete crackhead. Large crank craters (festering pusticles, aka boils) protruded in sharp relief on my face as the toxic chemical cocktail sought an outlet. Multiple outlets. I didn't have a T-zone, I had a war zone. I was a human metaphor for the city of Auckland — a volcanic field with nine live craters. I could be the city mascot.

I crouched on the floor, malnourished and dehydrated, bitter and twisted, paranoid and peering through a curtain of lank, greasy rats-tails. Stabbing pains ripped through my heart when I breathed, like the Witch King's knife in Frodo's chest. I would try to not breathe until I was sure they had gone. I asked Mark whether he got them, but he didn't. He wasn't worried, so neither was I, and I shrugged it off.

More than the obvious physical changes, the most shocking devastation was mental and emotional. The very essence of who I was had completely deserted me. Agreed, this had been pretty flaky to begin with, but now I was like a praying mantis when it turns from fluorescent green to insipid yellow, then just goes into a coma. I was in a prison of my own making.

This is what you're left with (if you're still alive) after two hard years slamming meth. And believe me, it could have been much worse.

> If only my anguish could be weighed and all my
> misery be placed on the scales! *Job 6:2*

Roy the printer did a double-take at my interpretation of a geeked-out drug addict when he called by the studio later that night. In fact, I think he thought I was someone else. He was right. I was someone else. I was a user. A user of people, a black hole with motives and an insatiable appetite that sucked everything into it and left nothing but emptiness. No one went to see a friend just to ask how he was. They went to see about an earn, or to get on it. No matter how good we got at disguising our motives, we were locusts, devouring everything in our path, then moving on to the next supply.

Roy's double-take turned over in my head as I wrestled to distinguish reality from paranoia. Wow, this is it. I'm about as low as a tweaker would want to get, and still know it. In a rare moment of clarity I saw myself as Roy saw me now. I could still remember fragments of who I had been. I saw the chasm of incongruence that now lay between the two versions of myself. It was the Grand Canyon. This black life marked by confrontation and random acts of violence just got uglier and more bizarre by the minute. Mark's heavy gold rings and the element of surprise were weapons. In a misguided kind of way I always felt safe when I was with him.

I felt safe, but I wasn't. I was blind to the spirit of death that stalked us.

> The waves of death swirled about me; the torrents of
> destruction overwhelmed me. *2 Samuel 22:5*

I couldn't completely give myself over to the dark side. The prayers being offered up on my behalf saw to that. I felt embarrassed and sad for the victims of violence or verbal abuse along the way. I was torn halfway between the dark side and the force, unable to fit in anywhere properly. Two years had passed since Gilda had attempted to save me from myself. This was one nasty mess.

I decided at that moment, I had to change. But how? What do you do when you've laid hold of the things you thought would make you happy, but they have become a spade in your hand that digs a hole so deep you can't crawl out or see light at the top? I wanted to leave but was simply unable. Change, loneliness, and the unknown were scarier than the familiar.

⟡⟡⟡

People around us were turning to crap as well. A friend of Mark's crashed his bike one night after a party at Silverdale. His lady came off ok that time but his face and leg were so wrecked I couldn't hide my shock next time I saw him, no matter how hard I tried. This big man was now unrecognisable, and hobbled painstakingly with a walking stick.

The next time he argued with the road, the road won. His lady survived, just. He didn't. Visiting her in the neurological ward I still couldn't see how easily it could have been me. We'd come from the same town. I used to babysit her kids when I was still a schoolgirl. We lived the same life. I bumped into her out shopping one day a few years later. She looked ok but it had been a long road to recovery, in every way. I knew the scars she carried. She'd lost two husbands to the 'lifestyle.'

Drone army: 2, Outlaws: Nil (still). Maybe the drones were onto something after all.

My people are destroyed from lack of knowledge.
Hosea 4:6

"Hi. I'm Janet, remember?" I said to her. I began to cry. I cried and cried and just couldn't stop. She looked at me with surprise.

"It's ok," she said.

"I'm just so sorry," I sobbed. It was anything but ok. I was overcome with grief and the hopelessness of it all. There were many casualties in this urban war, and there still are. Most go unnoticed by everyone but the devastated families and friends. They are just cold statistics and faceless names to a nation numbed by the magnitude of the problems we face today. Our psychological skin has been so cauterised we don't really care much anymore and build walls around our hearts for our own survival. Pass the salt, please.

∼ઔଓ ઔଓ∼

Mark and I had a love/hate relationship. Sometimes I hated him so much I thought about falling off the back of the bike on purpose just to make him feel bad. But I knew he wouldn't feel bad. He'd just say, "Stupid bitch." One day my dream almost came true.

The Harris pipes amped the noise and the power on Mark's sleek, black Softail Evo. The bike was loud, and Mark's riding style unapologetic. It was a beautiful bike but lacked one thing, a pillion seat. Things got interesting when cracking the ton and we were airborne, but I didn't lose my pillow. What I did nearly lose was my head when the wind caught my over-sized helmet. We were way down the line somewhere. There had been a problem with the starter motor this day. Mark kicked it over onto the ground and spat big boogers over it. It finally cranked to life.

"I'm not stopping, so if you want a ride back you'll have to get on when I ride past."

Since I didn't want to walk home from Taranaki, I made sure I got it right first time. By the time I'd sorted my pillow out, we were going as fast as we possibly could on the windy, narrow road. Mark didn't ease off the gas until we were out in front of the boys. I was just starting to relax into the ride when suddenly an enormous force almost snatched me off the bike. Automatically I grabbed my coat and wrenched it from the back wheel with all my strength. My long coat had come loose from under my butt. It was close. Mark noticed something happened but it didn't warrant a special stop. When we eventually took a pit stop I surveyed the damage. I looked as though I'd been in a shipwreck and shark attack on the same day.

"Man, look at my coat! It got caught in the wheel."

"Oh I thought I felt something pulling." Mark looked at me sideways, shaking his head.

I was totally unaware of the divine intervention it took to keep me alive, the prayers and the grace.

I was more gutted at losing my coat than almost losing my life.

For it is written: "He will command his angels concerning you to guard you carefully." *Luke 4:10*

❦

By now I'd clearly fallen right out of Maslow's box and was lying underneath it. During my revelation on the floor of the tattoo studio, I'd woken up and seen myself. I couldn't stand what I'd seen, and wanted to change instantly. I wanted to climb back into the box and join the drones again, to get back into the box and climb the rungs to the top. According to Maslow, when I reached the top I would be happy.

Understanding the depth of the crap I was in and the length of time, amount of effort and pain it was going to take to dig out, was crushing. I felt I would suffocate if I had to live one more day like this. But in reality it was going to take a long time of making small, but difficult choices to slowly change things. I'd been out of the workforce for a couple of years and was out of touch. Worse, my confidence had completely gone, and that's putting it mildly. I began with office temp work, then picked up some regular office work, ironically typing résumés for a recruitment agency. It took every ounce of courage I could muster. It was a slow and shaky process, but it was the start of building a life again.

We moved out of the tattoo studio into a tiny flat in Avondale, definitely another move in the right direction. It was good not to be sponging off mates; and this made a huge improvement to my emotional state. My conscience was starting to twitch again. Just a little.

Sitting in the lavatory cubicle at work, I had just found a vein, a miracle in itself, and injected some meth. That was better. Back to normal. I was a functioning drug addict. It cost as much to keep me in meth for the workday as I earned in a day's work, not counting cannabis or cigarettes, but I didn't see that as a problem because I didn't pay for it. My veins had taken such a hammering over the past two years, I just looked at a needle now and they disappeared. Scar tissue lined the insides of my favourite veins in layers. They were lumpy and uneven and very sore to inject into. This was

60

the first time I'd injected myself. Mark always did it for me.

"I'm saving you from yourself. Once you know how to do it yourself, it's all over," he had told me. I wasn't sure what had changed, but one day he felt generous and gave me some gear to take to work to blast. I'd taken another step. A step too far.

Back at home, Mark was doing the math. He came to a decision.

"We can't afford for us to both be drug addicts. Here's the plan. You give up first, then help me give up," he proposed.

I laughed. "Wow, that's big of you."

"Na, hang on," he said. "I'll make it worth your while. Here's the plan. Because you have to keep working while you're giving up, I'll make it easy for you. I'll put you up in a hotel for a week, close to work so you can walk. That way you don't have to worry about buses. Every day at lunch, you can go shopping and find something you like, a new outfit. Choose what you want, put it aside at the counter, and I'll go in the next day and get it for you. When you've cracked it, you can help me give up."

Well now, that was worth thinking about. I agreed. Mark had already chosen a hotel on Anzac Avenue. The next day I was moving into my new room. Breakfast was nice, downstairs, all laid out, no dishes to worry about, then off for a short walk to work. Monday went well, Tuesday went well. Wednesday didn't. This was rehab. I was done. I wasn't going to work and I didn't care if I lost my job. I was on my last warning so that would have been it. Mark made encouraging noises, talked me through it and got me going. I made it to work. Not happy, but I made it to work. It was rough.

When you don't have any money, you always see things you like in the shops. When you do have money, and especially when you only have less than an hour to buy, there is nothing in the shops you like. I was stressed and in withdrawal, running from shop to shop, desperately trying to find that outfit that would make everything ok. That would fill the hole. My reward. I went back to work empty-handed. Thursday was better. Friday was my last day at the hotel.

How was I going to cope without having my meals cooked, washing done and room tidied? Mark had gone and collected all the items I'd chosen and I felt like a queen. I could handle living like this. I needed longer. I didn't get longer. It was back to the real world, with a thump, minus one ravenous beast of a meth habit. So far, the plan had worked. It was a miracle.

I'd kept my end of the bargain; now I expected Mark to keep his.

⁕⊙⊙⁕

Mark disappeared for days at a time sometimes to tend his dope patches. "We're going over to the island on the boat. I want you to come," he said one day.

"Who's going?" I asked.

"A few of the guys and their girls."

My stomach sank.

"I don't want to go."

"I want you to come," he repeated.

He'd never asked me to go along before. It must have been some sort of attempt at cover. Being stuck on a boat together for a couple of days with some of the girls made solitary confinement look like a day at the spa. They were nice really, or as nice as you could be to 'the other woman', but this whole situation was giving me a nervous breakdown. However, codependency saw my yellow praying-mantis lips move weakly.

"Ok."

Going anywhere at all with Mark had become a nightmare. I was paranoid about who would be there, and what would they think and say to me. I tried to avoid situations when I didn't know who would be there and I was hyper-vigilant when some of them were there. Some hated me openly, some were curious but distant, some were nice but only to gain information that could be used against me. A rare few were genuinely nice.

This all created incredible strain. I tried to get out of going anywhere because of stress and fear. I cowered at home on Mark's 40th birthday and Mark's daughter, Danielle's birthdays bound by fear of people, and hurting the ones I loved. People thought I was just a bitch and didn't care, and I was judged and disliked even more. I was damned if I did, and damned if I didn't. It all made my head and heart hurt and fuelled my paranoia, which didn't need any encouragement. My symptoms were approaching those of a post-traumatic stress disorder and had started to drive a wedge between Mark and me. My mental anguish was amplified by my own vote being with the haters. I was one of the biggest. A thick heaviness cloaked me, a heaviness of heart, mind and soul. The early years were rough.

We left Auckland like any other boat and motored out into the Hauraki Gulf. It was a party boat and everyone got straight down to it. I still didn't drink alcohol. Most people didn't share my enthusiasm for this particular lifestyle choice, even though I'd stuck to it for nearly ten years now. Some reacted as if I'd just done it to piss them off. Some would ask if I wanted a drink. I'd say "Yes, please, I'll have a lemonade thanks." They'd look at me blankly and make a note to self that said, 'No, she doesn't want a drink,' and forget I'd said anything. Being a non-drinker around a bunch of drinkers is like watching the Teletubbies for hours on end — the best way I know to completely do your head in. I got as stoned as possible to numb the pain, but this aggravated the paranoia. Communication would get twisted and often tipped over into real demonic interference.

Soon, everyone was wasted, even the captain. The call went out for crayfish even though the sea was too rough. A fairly large swell played with the boat until we finally came down on the rocks. Holding our breaths, we looked at each other with wide eyes, but luckily the next wave unhooked us. A collective sigh of relief. We laughed. Incredibly there was no damage to the hull. But there was a storm brewing in more ways than one. I hated every minute. Eyeing the girls with distrust they eyed me back with dislike. No surprises there.

We finally arrived and anchored as close as we could to land so the guys could ferry their gear to shore. They bailed for the mission, leaving just one who was too wasted to go. As time went on, tension on the boat escalated, and things went from unpleasant to downright ugly. I counted down the seconds for the guys to come back and save us from ourselves.

Without warning, the paralytic decided he'd take the boat for a spin. He pulled up anchor and floored it hard. We careered dangerously straight toward shore. He hadn't noticed we were facing land and were already too shallow to go any further in. In fact, beaching ourselves would have been for the best. As it was, we were also heading straight for the side of another vessel. The people on the other boat saw us coming at them full noise and jumped up and down, shouting for us to turn and slow down. At the very last second, the clown woke up and wrenched the wheel to the left. We missed the boat by a whisker.

When the guys finally emerged from the bush the next day, we all breathed a sigh of relief. They were loaded down with huge sacks of cannabis and tools. After dumping the weed in the hold with their gear, the boat rode so low in the water I wondered how we'd get home without sinking. Surely, we must be running low on lives by now. The smell of the weed in the hold was phenomenal. After a big session, we set off in a puff of smoke. As we chugged heavily toward the mainland, diesel fumes grew stronger and stronger until they became almost life-threatening. Just before we all passed out, someone decided to investigate. The hungry sea had eaten the exhaust.

Just when we thought it couldn't get any worse, the motor shuddered to a stop and we ran out of fuel. We dropped anchor but were too deep and the wind was too strong, and were blown towards the coastline like a rubber ducky, dragging anchor. There was no option. With a boat full of illegal poundage, we put through the S.O.S. to the Coastguard. The S.O.S. that went up from my own soul, however, was more urgent. If I hadn't been so worried, I would have injured myself laughing.

"This is it. We're done." For once, opinion was unanimous. Even if the Coastguard didn't come on board, they would fully smell the gear from their vessel. We reeked for miles.

I sweated bullets and fought waves of nausea from stress and a diesel headache as the Coastguard towed us into port. Incredibly, our dirty secret was never discovered.

The difference between stupidity and genius is that genius has its limits.
Albert Einstein

"There you go — better luck next time," the Coastguard said, waving a cheery goodbye.

"Yea, thanks very much!" said Mark, smiling and waving.

DL Moody noted that our greatest fear should not be that we succeed or fail at something. Our greatest fear should be that we succeed at something that doesn't matter. I was beginning to understand what he was getting at.

"Next time, you're on your own!" I announced. This parody of my life was not my idea of fun.

My resolution, however, was short-lived. When next time came, I was there.

What good is it for someone to gain the whole world, yet forfeit their soul? *Mark 8:36*

❧ ❧

6. Shattered

1998

"You can drive," Mark said to me.

"Where to?"

We'd just pulled up outside a large patch of cannabis in broad daylight. Mark and his mate grabbed sacks out of the back of the pickup. Mark popped his head back into the cab.

"Watch and wait. Be ready. You drive when we get back," he said.

My heart was thumping painfully. Oh man. "Ok," I said, sliding into the driver's seat. The guys ran to the patch, ripped large plants from the ground one after the other, row after row. Soon the huge sacks were full. Mark knew they were being watched. They moved with speed and purpose, in and out as quickly as possible up and down rows. When they'd filled as many sacks as they could drag in one go, the back of the pickup sagged low as the guys heaved the mother lode onto the back. They took a few seconds to crudely fasten a tarp over the sticky heap.

"GO!" Mark barked as they leapt into the cab. I floored it. My mouth went dry as I realised I had to drive through the city to get where we were going.

I noticed some movement in the rear vision mirror. Some of the buds had sprung loose and had popped up around the edges of the tarp in a Mexican wave. Long branches heavy with heads were waving to the passersby, shouting look at me! When we stopped at the lights, I refused to look at the person in the lane beside me. I was on thin ice. The smell engulfed the pickup and surrounding vehicles as we stopped. The heaviness of stinky skunk made it hard to breathe and made our eyes water. If you could see the smell, it would look like an Aussie dust storm, but green, engulfing everything in its path. It was impossible to ignore even if you didn't know what it was.

There were no cops around. We made it back to base without being snapped. The city around us had gone blind and unable to smell as we passed through in our own micro-climate of smog. It reminded me of Captain Spears in Band of Brothers, running right in front of the Germans to hook up with I Company, then back again right in front of their eyes. Except we weren't the heroes. Something deep down inside hated being on the wrong team, but another part loved the thrill. When I didn't hate Mark, I loved him so much I couldn't imagine living without him. This was just the way it was. Well over the edge, all the time. We were invincible.

At least for a while I thought we were.

But I was wrong.

Such are the paths of all who go after ill–gotten gain; it takes away the life of those who get it.
Proverbs 1:19

ঌগ্ন ৩েেᴑ

Demonic activity was rife in our lives, and my nightmares were something else. I was getting worried. I visited an elderly couple I knew who performed exorcisms. They didn't want to help, and the fear I saw on their faces freaked me out. At my wit's end, I rang a Christian ministry.

"I need help. We're being bothered by evil spirits."

"Are you living in sin?"

"What?"

"Are you living in sin?"

"Well, my boyfriend and I are living together," I said, wondering if that was what he meant.

"Are you prepared to stop living in sin, and get your life in order?"

"No."

"You're doomed!"

"Eh?"

End of conversation. He was right, but this approach was of little help to me at that moment. There I was, still searching for answers, holding the phone in my hand. I wasn't prepared or even able to 'get my life in order' to free myself of what was hassling us. I really didn't know what that meant, what was so wrong about it, didn't have the strength or courage to 'stop living in sin', and had no one to talk to about it. Why did it have to be so difficult? Did I have to leave my partner, or get married to be rid of these demons? I just didn't get it.

My cry for help went unanswered, so I embraced my normal way of coping once again. We pulled up outside the needle exchange in Symonds Street to get some new picks. I went in, got sorted and ran down the stairs. I was pumped at the thought of another blast of P. My bubble was unceremoniously popped the second my foot hit the street. The car was alive with cops. I looked at Mark.

"What the!"

He shrugged. I couldn't understand it. I was only gone a minute.

"Make yourself at home!" I said to an officer's butt that protruded out of the boot. A shout of victory went up as a cop held up the Beretta from the driver's door pocket. Another triumphant crow as another cop pulled the other handgun from the glove box. The guns were gone but that was where it stopped. In their zeal the cops had made classic dumb cop mistake 101: no search warrant.

We had moved out of the Avondale flat and our new place was a derelict old building just up the road from the needle exchange. With 1,500 square feet to spread out in, one thing we finally had tons of was room. Before long, Mark had it fully decked out. A full-sized slate snooker table took pride of place, animal heads and weapons decorated the walls, and large potted palms brought life into the realm of the dead. A security camera system, peep-hole in the door and several locks were compulsory. This was our Helm's Deep.

Mark surveyed his domain. He decided he wanted a front for his drug business and Paradox Graphics was born. I brought the recruitment résumé work home and that formed the base for my freelance secretarial service out of Paradox so my modus operandi wouldn't be disrupted — smoking dope and getting wasted.

Mark's friend, Micha, was a graphic designer; and he brought in his Apple Mac. I watched as he played on his computer. He used it to make art. My eyes were opened to a whole new world. I'd only used PCs and seen them pump out screeds of boring words and flowcharts. I stood behind Micha, my eyes bugging out and my heart pounding as he created masterpieces and had fun in Photoshop. I was standing on the edge of a new frontier; of a whole new world so large I couldn't see where it ended. The only limit was my imagination. It was overwhelming. I was looking through a window into a new life. My future.

It wasn't long before Micha's playing shifted to creating counterfeit $100 notes, just in time for the next police raid.

⁕⁕⁕

I was working my butt off madly typing résumés. Mark had ridden his Harley up the two flights of wide stairs and was working on it while I typed. The pressure was starting to bite. I had too much work and I needed a hand.

"Mark, can you drop these résumés off for me when I've finished, and pick up the next lot? I'm snowed under. I'm too busy to do the running around and the typing."

"Ok. Just let me know when you're ready," he said, not looking up. Cool. That was awesome as I was getting quite stressed.

A while later I was ready. "Ok. You're good to go now," I told him.

"Do it yourself. I'm busy."

"F*@king asshole," I snarled. I grabbed the keys to the BMW and the pile of reports and headed out the door. It's not the things we worry about that generally do the damage in our lives. It's the ones that blindside us out of the blue. By the time I came back from my short trip, our lives would be turned upside down.

The godless in heart harbour resentment; even
when he fetters them, they do not cry for help.
Job 36:13

As soon as the traffic light turned green, I floored it. *SMASH!* It was
practically a head-on as some loser ran the red and drove straight into me.
The impact was huge.

First, shock, then rage. I was going to smash his head in, whoever had
done this evil thing. I was going to smash and smash and smash until I felt
strong enough to take whatever was coming my way now, because of him.
His bad day was about to get a whole lot worse. I was going to hit and hit
and hit until I was happy, and that would take a while. I got out and went
hunting. I found him cowering in his car. He turned his head to look at
me. My heart dropped. There was no point at all. There was no point in
smashing him because he was already as pathetic as he could get, emaciated
and haunted. His mate was the same. I saw the dirty mattress in the back of
their Lada and shuddered.

A couple of witnesses ran up to me "I saw it happen! It was his fault.
Here's my number, I'll be a witness for you," they said, putting their cards
in my hand.

"Thanks."

Somewhere deep down I was worried. I knew it made no difference
that the accident wasn't my fault. In Mark's eyes, it was simple. His car was
wrecked and I'd been driving. It was my fault.

"You're coming with us," the ambulance attendant said to me, taking me
by the arm. "If you were in that car, you must have neck injuries. There's
no way you can't be hurt. We'll get you checked out at hospital," he said
fastening a brace around my neck.

No! That's the least of my problems, I wanted to scream. I was
inconsolable. Mark had asked me to insure the BMW but I'd been so busy I
hadn't got around to it. The hospital staff told me it was going to be ok, but
once again, I knew it wasn't. Upon my release, I got a taxi back to Paradox,
trying to control my panic as I went inside. Mark wasn't there. He was at the
tow-yard making sure his car was going to pull through. I walked down to

the tow-yard in my neck brace. He glared at me.

"Twenty grand worth of damage," were his first words to me.

Even the neck brace seemed to anger him; a sign of weakness. He looked at the guy who'd hit me.

"You're coming back to my office to talk. You owe me a lot of money," he said, shoving the guy and his scrawny friend to get them moving. A few minutes later, they sat in front of Mark's desk with their eyes bugging out. What the hell was this place? Whatever it is, it can't be good.

"What do you do?" Mark asked the guy. Single syllable words were appropriate.

"I've just got a part-time job at a burger bar in Hamilton."

Oh my gosh, I knew it. We're screwed.

"That's it?" said Mark. "Well how do you plan to pay for this?"

"I don't know," said Crash.

"Where are your parents?"

"My Dad lives in Thames."

"You can ring from here and tell him what you've done," Mark said. He wanted a point of contact when this little flea disappeared the second he hit the street.

"He's not on the phone."

"Well you'll have to go and see him then," Mark said.

"Oh."

Mark picked up the phone and dialled a friend to get a ride, seeing both our cars were wrecked. That guy was busy. He dialled another. That one was busy too. The third guy wasn't. But he was busy acclimatising after being released from prison. A giant of a man, Kane had just been released on compassionate grounds near the end of a ten-year sentence for aggravated robbery and murder. Next time, he said, he'd use a pen instead of a gun when he went to withdraw money from the bank. The miserable pair sat together, knees knocking and chain-smoking.

Mark barked at me. "I'm not going. You did it. You sort it out." This came as no surprise at all. "Take this," he said, handing me a walking stick. I stared at it blankly. He took it back and pulled the handle out. A very long thin blade withdrew from the scabbard. That was tricky. Crash's eyes bugged a bit further. I took it. Just in case.

Thinking this would be a good time to desert his friend, Crash's mate piped up, "I've got to get going now."

Mark looked at him with dislike. "Go. The door is open." He was off like a robber's dog without a backward glance, revealing a cigarette burn on the seat where he'd been. Mark hated cigarettes. Mark zeroed in on Crash, eyes narrowing. He handed him a pad and pen. "You can write all the names and phone numbers of your family so I've got somewhere to go when you flea off."

The guy started writing, his knuckles white. The list was short. Mark ripped off the piece of paper and stuffed it into his pocket.

"Get going."

Kane, Crash and I left for Thames on a mission to find the guy's father. It was a mission of accountability. Doing our best to keep Crash comfortable, we offered chocolate and drinks, but by the time we got to Thames he was a little green.

We pulled up to Crash's family home. My heart dropped like a brick on a big toe. Hope of obtaining accountability or anything else from this trip, or from Crash, evaporated. Crash's latest incident was obviously the just another day in the life. I shuddered.

We are foreigners and strangers in your sight, as were all our ancestors. Our days on earth are like a shadow, without hope. *1 Chronicles 29:15*

I'd seen trash dumps before, but nothing like this. The place looked as though the Munsters had lived there, but now, even they had gone. The derelict building leaned on a slight angle as if it were only standing because of the spiders and termites holding hands. It was laughing at us. The paint had almost finished peeling off and was mostly down to bare wood. The windows were black. The grounds were a wilderness of old rubbish and wild vegetation.

"He's not home," said Crash. 'Home' was not a word you would associate with this godforsaken dump. A new kind of pity for Crash fell upon me.

"Where would he be?" I asked.

"I don't know. Maybe at the pub."

"We've come all this way, we're not leaving till we find him." I was torn. Even though I felt sorry for Crash, he was my scapegoat. Either he was going to take the fall, or I was. And it wasn't going to be me. We pulled up at the pub. Kane waited in the wagon while I followed Crash inside with my new walking stick. People looked at us weirdly; the skinny guy with the girl following closer than a brother. The father was nowhere to be seen.

"I need to go to the toilet," Crash said.

"I'm coming with you," I said following him, to the punter's amazement. 'Be just like him to take off out the window', noted my inner narrator. Kane and I faced the facts. This was a joke. What a waste of a trip.

"We might as well go and have a coffee with Dave and Sue in Coromandel, mate. Save this trip from being a complete waste of time," I said to Kane. Our faithful friends had waved city life goodbye and gone bush. When we finally got done with the windy coast road, Crash was looking decidedly worse for wear. In fact, he made me sick to look at. He lurched out of the wagon pulling huge gasps of air into his sticky, tar-stained lungs as soon as we got to Dave and Sue's.

"You want to come in for a coffee?" I asked Crash.

"No. I'm going to wait here," he squeaked, peering at me warily, sagging against the station wagon.

'Yea, you do that, and take off as soon as our backs are turned,' I thought bitterly. I'd stopped caring if he did. Useless bastard had ruined my life. To my amazement, Crash was still there when we'd finished visiting Dave and Sue. When we arrived back at Paradox, Mark was not pleased but was graceful. Handing Crash a note with our phone number on it, Mark told him, "call me every two days and let me know how you're getting on finding the money. You'll just have to pay it off."

Crash took the number and bolted.

As I have observed, those who plough evil and those who sow trouble reap it. *Job 4:8*

☙ ❧

73

7. Busted

1998

The phone rang several days later. Mark picked it up. It was Crash.

"I haven't had any luck," he said.

"Well? Keep trying."

Silence.

"So, I suppose it's going to be really bad for me, if I don't come up with the money." Crash carried on with his blatantly leading series of statements.

"Keep trying. You can't be a loser all your life," Mark said calmly and hung up. Mark treated every phone call as if someone were listening. He knew the call was being taped. Sure enough, Crash was ringing from the cop shop. The police had been after Mark for a while. Now was their chance to use extortion and kidnapping as door-openers, and they were going to make the most of it. Each time Crash rang, it was the same. No good news and he supposed that meant things weren't going to go very well for him.

Mark vented fully on me for crashing the car. My misery and opinion of myself descended to new depths. It seemed right that he didn't care whether I was dead when he found out about the crash. I always was just one of his things, and the car was worth more. When he wasn't being mean to me, I was being mean to myself. I became more and more driven to work and earn money to help make things right. I spent my time cold-calling around the CBD to build our client base.

Preparing for a long anticipated interview with a major trading bank regarding new business, I was brushing my teeth in the bathroom. I looked good in my beautiful handmade Italian wool dress and high heels. I absently heard the knock on the door and thought nothing of it. The coveted appointment was exciting. I had already been forced to postpone it twice before for various reasons/unfortunate events, and not even Armageddon was going to stop me this time. I faced the mirror, mentally preparing for the meeting, toothbrush still working. Two policemen joined me in the reflection, one at each elbow. I kept calmly brushing my teeth as though it wasn't happening. Maybe they would just go away if I ignored them.

They spoke to my reflection, "You're coming with us." I failed to see the funny side.

"Oh no I'm not!" I said. "I've got a meeting to go to, and I'm not missing it."

"You're not going anywhere. You'll have to ring and cancel."

Fury filled my sails, *"Oh no I won't!"*

"We have a search warrant for documents relating to kidnapping."

I laughed out loud, relieved at the absurdity. "Well, you've got the wrong place," I said, thinking that would be it. Misunderstanding over. Crisis averted. Carry on people, there's nothing to see here. Go back to your normal lives. But I was wrong again. A search warrant for 'Documents relating to kidnapping' was produced, which promptly began with a personal search of Mark. It took less than two seconds to pull a couple of joints from his shirt pocket. It was just what they needed.

What followed was surreal. The frame rate dropped to slow motion as a cop opened the door and signalled to the drug squad who were waiting on the landing. A dozen cops poured into the place, complete with dogs, torches and ladders. Every drawer, box and bag was mechanically dumped upside down on the floor. This was getting out of control. Mark and I were separated and denied any chance of talking to each other.

At this stage, G decided now was a good time to visit. Missing all the cues outside, i.e., police vehicles, he stumbled right into Paradox in the middle of the action, just because things weren't crazy enough.

I made the call. "Hi, it's Janet here, sorry I won't be able to make our appointment today. I'm so sorry." And I was. I couldn't make it right because I was still making it wrong. How wrong, I couldn't even imagine. I watched the lips on the cop moving up and down as he read me my rights, then began his questioning. I knew full well the unwritten rule. Never say anything at all, ever, to a cop. But I was sure they would see it was a misunderstanding when I explained. There was no kidnapping. We had non-violently stood up for our rights. I mean, for goodness sake, we hadn't even punched the guy! We'd treated him nice! It was a miracle he'd walked away at all. I was starting to regret that he had. I spilled the lot, telling my side of the story at the risk of it all being used against me. I had nothing to hide. We were the victims.

"What were we supposed to do? What would you have done?" I demanded of the cop, seeking understanding.

"Have insurance," came the reply. Ahh! I wanted to scream, loud and long before fizzling out and leaving my empty shell lying on the floor like a discarded garment.

"You took the law into your own hands. You don't do that," he said, having tried us and found us guilty until proven innocent. Judge, jury and sad he wasn't executioner.

"It's a joke! The guy could have left at any time! The door was never locked. He was never tied up. He walked to our place under his own steam!"

"He was too scared to leave," came the automated response.

The memory of Crash came flooding back. His pathetic weakness sickened me to my guts then, but now it was worse. The guy just kept blowing me away with his yellowness. I wished once again, that I'd given him the appropriate first response and punched his head clean off. I'd feel a lot better now. I had so much anger built up inside, I never lived in fear of being a victim. Again I fantasised about hitting and hitting and hitting until there was nothing left.

Mark wasn't speaking of course. They realised they'd get nothing out of him, and he was taken into custody very quickly. He glanced over his shoulder as they led him away. His eyes said it all. Behind me was the mess, the dogs jumping all over his antique snooker table, the cannabis coming down the ladder from the ceiling, the methamphetamine, guns, cash and counterfeit notes. The stockpile of contraband was growing larger by the second.

"You assholes can pick all that up!" I screamed, as they finished tipping out a dozen boxes of my sewing gear.

The police were suspicious of one of my clients, an Asian trade facilitator, and thought they might be onto something big. If I hadn't been so pissed off it would have been funny. Everything was blown so out of proportion it was doing my head in. Can't they just leave us alone and get on with chasing the criminals? And why do they keep taking our freakin' stuff all the time? I was sure they wanted it for themselves.

The police gave Mark and me both barrels. Inspired by Crash's bullshit, they conjured up the kidnapping angle. Kidnapping carries a fourteen-year prison sentence. That would do for starters. By the time the day was finished, Mark and I were charged with fourteen offences each. Paradox was ransacked from top to bottom. Apart from the obvious, cash, computers and paperwork were also confiscated. The night spent at Auckland Central Police Station was less than salubrious.

Whoever walks in integrity walks securely, but whoever takes crooked paths will be found out. *Proverbs 10:9*

Fingerprints and mugshot taken; I was left alone with my narrator who rehearsed the maddening and the depressing like flies on a dunghill. I had work on my desk, deadlines to meet, meetings to go to and a business to build, not to mention the devastation to my nearest and dearest and my impending prison sentence. Losing the car was just the opener. Surely I was the worst thing that could have ever happened to Mark. Was I cursed? I swung wildly between hating Mark and hating myself. Hating how he deliberately hurt me. Hating how vicious I was to him. Selfishness and dissension reigned, so it follows that the bad times sometimes outnumbered the good. We had to replace plates and cups all the time. Whenever we had a smashing fit, we didn't stop until it was all gone.

If a house is divided against itself, that house cannot stand. *Mark 3:25*

The key turned in the lock.

"Get up."

I dully watched our place in Symonds Street pass by the paddy wagon portal. I arrived at my new home, Mount Eden Prison, still in my best dress and high heels. The butch old guard gave me the once-over. "Well, you can't wear that in here!" she said, shaking her head. The things some people wear to jail these days. No idea.

"Oh sorry, shall I go home and get changed?" I asked. I'd love to go home. And stay home. I wanted to undo this whole thing. Undo, undo, undo, undo! Oh how I wished Mark had done the delivery that day and not me. I wish, I wish, if only this, if only that. I wished my stupid life away.

My clothes and shoes stored away in a brown paper bag, I was treated to a bath with parasite shampoo, lest I contaminate the prisoners. Dressed in a clean set of prison couture, I clutched my small bag of creature comforts; toothbrush, toothpaste, comb and soap. I was ready to meet my new mates.

"Follow me!" Butch barked. Heart thumping loudly, I followed the she-man into a new realm. Progress was slow, stopping every few metres to unlock and lock gates on the way to the remand wing. My internal critic offered harsh narrative and rarely paused for breath. The 'girls' didn't acknowledge me as I was let into their cage. My cell nestled underneath spaghetti junction. The city's aorta pumped people about their business twenty-four seven as my world shrank around me like plastic wrap. A gate clanging in the distance had the last word. There was nothing I could do that I needed to do. No one to see that I wanted to see. I ventured out of my cell, preferring the possibility of being torn to shreds by rabid inmates than my own company.

"Hi," I said, mustering a sheepish smile. Nobody smiled back; nobody spoke. Well, clearly behaviour like that wasn't tolerated. I decided to drink a cup of concrete and harden up. My esteemed company included an arsonist, a dope-grower from up north, and a heroin addict punk with a large tattoo around her neck that screamed ALEX in neo-Nazi script. ALEX had no trouble getting gear in the big house.

Clanging gates heralded Butch's arrival the next day. "You wanna make a phone call?" With a deep breath, I made a call to sister Sam. We had ridden around the countryside together for miles and miles in the sunshine on our trusty steeds as kids. She had always been there for me, no matter what, which was quite something. When I gave her address to the police under pressure one day, unable to say where I was really staying, some of her house mates got slightly busted. Sam gave me a flash of the steely blues and 'the tone', but the love never skipped a beat.

"Hi."

"Hi."

"How are you?"

"Good. Work's busy."

"Yea. I'm in jail."

"What? What for?"

"Oh, it's a long story, but hopefully I'll get out on bail soon. Don't tell Mum and Dad." No pressure.

I didn't know what else to do. I dumped the horrible news on her then told her to keep it from the only people who would want to know and could share the burden. Mum used to pump Sam for years for information about what was going on with me. Intensely loyal and trustworthy to the end, eventually Mum realised she was never ever going to get a word out of Sam, and gave up. I appreciated the moral support. Mum puts it like this:

Jan is like the grand rapids, rushing along at great speed and energy, crashing into rocks and tumbling over drops; while Sam is the quiet pool, still and unfathomable, quiet, but with great depth.

ৡৡ ৡৡ

Where can I go from your Spirit? Where can I flee from your presence? If I go up to the heavens, you are there; if I make my bed in the depths, you are there. *Psalm 139:7-8*

Back in the remand wing after my phone call, an old nun was visiting. She brought wool so the girls could knit. I like knitting, but man, come on!

They were too tough to smile or answer, but they knitted? ALEX looked at me.

"Do you know how to cast on?"

"Um," I stalled, thinking, 'I sure hope so!'

I panicked. I was going to cop a bash, because I couldn't cast on? Then I remembered. I couldn't cop a bash because I had so much canned fury I could fight anyone. I relaxed.

"Yea, I think I can remember," I took the needles and wool from her.

"You only need one needle to cast on." Mum's voice was coming back to me. As I held the needle and threaded the wool over my thumb, I was a young girl back at home listening to my mother's instruction as my fingers worked. ALEX smiled and grunted thanks as I handed her the knitting. The nun finished chatting to the dope grower and came to see me. "Hello dear. Do you mind if we have a chat?"

"Ok."

"Does your mother know you're here, dear?" she enquired gently.

"No. And I don't want her to know."

"Oh. Then I hope she doesn't find out." I appreciated her respect for my wishes and her ability to really listen.

"Here's some rosary beads and a necklace, if you would like them." I held the cross and ran the pale blue satin ribbon through my fingers.

I took the gifts from the old nun and felt comfort on an unfamiliar level. I didn't know how to bridge the gap to the one who could help, the one who is closer than a brother, but he was there anyway. He worked through Sam. He worked through the nun. He even worked through ALEX.

That's grace.

I will strengthen you, though you have not acknowledged me, so that from the rising of the sun to the place of its setting people may know there is none besides me. I am the Lord, and there is no other. *Isaiah 45:5-6*

News came that a friend was trying to break into Paradox to get our passports that we needed for the bail application, in time for the weekend. Mark's parents kindly posted the $100,000 cash for bail. My heart leapt at the news of our release. Our only concerns were getting stoned and running the legal rat race set before us.

The bail conditions were a prison in themselves, and it was ages until our case came to trial. We were required to check in every day at Auckland Central Police Station between the hours of 4 p.m and 5 p.m; not to speak to any criminals (our friends); not go beyond a radius of 5 kilometres from Auckland Central Police Station at any time; and to appear in court when summoned. I've heard of murderers whose bail conditions were less than half as strict. Any breach of these conditions, and the $100,000 posted by Marks' parents would be forfeit. No pressure.

The cops had thrown the book at both of us. Mark was charged with two counts of kidnap for gain, as they included Crash's friend as well. All charges were lumped onto me too, in the hope that Mark would spill all to get me off the hook, a common tactic.

Mark played ball and accepted responsibility for the guns and drugs, et cetera I was charged with. He told them I had nothing to do with any of it, he denied the counterfeiting as this was Micha's gig, and of course the kidnapping was a complete joke. My extraneous charges were dropped, leaving me with just one charge of kidnapping to answer. Crash was given a pat on the back for running the red and handing them Mark on a plate, and he didn't pay reparation for the vehicle he hit. He was kitted out with a new wardrobe for court to make him look credible, a new identity, and a new life in Australia under a witness-protection scheme. All this in an effort to sensationalise the case and blow it out of proportion for effect, as had been with the disproportionate bail. It was a win for Crash.

After this minor hiccup, I picked up where I'd left off with the long-suffering recruitment agency, freelancing back at their offices once again through Paradox. One day, shortly after our release on bail I was at work, fingers flying across the keyboard. A workmate appeared beside my desk. I didn't stop typing.

"Hey Janet, have you seen the paper today?"

"No," I said, wondering why she thought I would be interested in reading the country's largest newspaper.

"There's an article about you on the second page."

My fingers slowed and came to rest on the keyboard. She laid the aforementioned article out on my desk so I could feast my eyes upon it. It said something about three Aucklanders having been charged with a couple of crimes, and one of them had the same name as me. The charges were for drugs, counterfeiting, possession of forged banknotes, demanding with menaces and threatening to kill, alleged kidnapping, unlawful possession of a .308 rifle, a .55 Colt semi-automatic pistol and a 9mm Ruger pistol, possession of methamphetamines for supply, possession of cannabis for supply, and possession of cannabis, and so on and so forth.

I had just enough time to read it before being summoned to the boss's office. Shit. I made my way in slow motion to see The Boss. Memories of the recent marketing day surfaced. Images returned of us dressed as Cowboys, Indians or Dolly Partons if you preferred, as our teams vied to bring in the most new clients. My authentic cowboy costume had won me a giant can of baked beans. The costume with the real gun belt loaded with live ammunition and a real pistol. I was feeling the loss of the toys. And the car. My boss was struggling to see the funny side.

"They're just allegations! It's a misunderstanding," I offered weakly, petering out at the end.

That particular day I was given the benefit of the doubt, and a very short leash.

The year dragged by, ruled by bail conditions that hung over us like a low black cloud. I moved from the recruitment agency to working at a stock brokerage firm in the research department. It was a busy job but every day at the same time I had to down tools and mysteriously pop out. Some days, checking in wasn't a problem but others, traumatic, especially with no car. Fear of losing Mark's parents' hundred grand was a ferocious motivator.

Mark had days when he just slept, too depressed to rise. Still, I'd wake him up to check in, and endure the wrath. A new heaviness of heart had fallen upon us. I had kept my part of the bargain, giving up meth. Now I expected Mark to keep his end. He didn't.

If this was karma, I didn't like it. Something had changed in the cosmos. Things weren't working for us anymore. I had a tangible feeling of swimming against the tide.

I set my face like flint and gave myself permission to die trying.

Whoever digs a hole and scoops it out falls into the pit they have made. *Psalm 7:15*

8. Paradox

1998

The days of Paradox were just that. As soon as we were released on bail the police had us evicted from our Symonds Street address. We had very little time to find a new place. Mark went to bed until further notice, and I was left to find a way forward. We moved into a commercial building a couple of blocks away in East Street, Newton. This was smack, bang in the middle of the 'sick circuit,' a questionable part of town at the back of Karangahape Road where cars with men in good suits circled their prey like sharks. Solvent-sniffing, drug-addicted trans-gender prostitute territory.

The rebuild of Paradox began. These premises were large, open plan and had a heartbeat, unlike the corpse we had just left, and a lot more expensive. A real commitment considering we were looking down the barrel of jail time, but we had little choice. Mark had so much gear we had to take what we could get. It had to go somewhere, and so did we.

We sub-leased part of the premises to Mark's friend, Roy, an offset printer. Paradox Graphics was never meant to be anything more than a front for Mark's drug interests, however, I needed to redeem myself. Determined to grow a legitimate business, I threw myself into building a client base.

Mark performed reconstructive surgery on the home and office. His advertising expertise and print contacts were vast, having grown up in his parents successful typographical services company. I hung around Micha as he did his graphics, and learned. He was a fantastic teacher, and there was much to know. Just add on-the-job experience working with Roy, and I had a new trade. Graphic design.

ຈຸ®ໂ໑ໂຈຸ

Eventually, the day came. We rocked up to court for the deposition's hearing. The tables in front of the court groaned under the weight of the physical exhibits. It was decided we had a case to answer, and eventually the case was heard. Mark received a six-year jail sentence for the combined total of his charges to be run concurrently. This meant Mark only had to serve time for the longest of any single charge. Two years.

"Ms. Balcombe, you've been found guilty of 'Detaining with Consent, Under Duress', and are hereby sentenced to carry out one hundred hours of Community Service," the judge dribbled.

Our kidnapping charges were reduced to 'detaining with consent, under duress,' as they knew their kidnapping proposal would never hold water. I notice, however, that my criminal record declares, 'kidnaps for gain'. Mark was led away to begin his sentence in Kaitoki Prison.

"Kaitoki? Where the hell is that?" I croaked, visibly shaking. Kaitoki Prison was down the bottom of the North Island near Whanganui, aka the South Pole. Outrage at Crash's getting away with murdering Mark's car and triggering all that followed, boiled over. "But he was never locked in or tied up at any time. We even left him alone outside for an hour and a half in Coromandel," whined my inner victim.

"The prosecution argued it was a psychological detainment. He was too scared to leave," the lawyer said patiently.

"But I'm only a girl, and he's a guy!" I said, forgetting about the incredible hulk who drove us.

"He said, 'But she had a cellphone!'" our lawyer answered. Yea and I knew how to use it. My conscience gave me a nudge. Just as well he'd forgotten about the 'walking stick'. Maybe I'd better not push my luck after all. My bias had caused convenient amnesia.

Our beautiful friend May Cowan, knew it was going to be rough. Experienced herself at helping people in court, she was with us every step of the way. Walking back into Paradox after court, reality punched me right in the guts. No more Mark. No more cash to bridge Paradox's shortfalls. The burden was crushing the breath out of me. I couldn't bear to think any further than the next rent. The cords of codependency were stretched to breaking point.

This was my worst nightmare so far. Deep down in my heart of hearts dwelt a persistent desire to help people. I didn't know how, but I wanted to help people. The disparity between my reality and my heart's desire couldn't have been more extreme. I wanted to be part of the solution, not part of the problem. I wanted to be at the top of Maslow's chart, not at the bottom! When I shared my dream about helping people I saw the laughter dance in their eyes. It just sounded ridiculous from where I was sitting.

But still, the desire remained.

For we are God's handiwork, created in Christ Jesus to do good works, which God prepared in advance for us to do. *Ephesians 2:10*

Paradox struggled for repeat business. What we needed were solid clients who would use us for all their needs. Before Mark went to jail, I'd regularly temped for an international investment bank where Pete and another member of the GAE team, Wozza, now worked. However, now I felt the need to work from Paradox and build the graphics business properly.

One day after sitting at Paradox working on stuff that wasn't going to pay, my frustration boiled over. I marched straight down to the research department and hit them up about some work. Literally. I stood next to Wozza and looked at the report he was working on. Then I picked it up and hit him over the head with it a couple of times.

"Why the bloody hell won't you give me some work?" I demanded. Pete looked at us and laughed. They both knew what I was like. It was hard to believe I'd completed the Dale Carnegie course, 'How to Win Friends and Influence People'.

"I should give you this, shouldn't I?" Wozza smiled, snatching the report.

"Yes, you should!" I said, rolling my eyes. This was the unlikely beginning of a six-year business relationship.

With Micha's expertise, we modernised the bank's printing, taking it from old-school to digital. They emailed me their reports and I designed the covers, imposed their reports for print and managed the printing and delivery. Their work was delivered sooner and looked better than ever.

Later on, Paradox published New Zealand's first tattoo and body art magazine for Tattoo Phill. We produced the first and second issues, and taught Phill graphics. He put the third issue out himself on his own computer. There were some challenges and the third was the last.

"You remind me of a bird in a gilded cage," Phill shrewdly observed one day.

I worked hard to occupy my mind, but the ache of missing Mark refused to be placated. Mark's mates popped in often to visit and have a coffee and a joint with me. I had only one friend with whom I maintained a friendship. Over the years, whatever had given value and meaning to life had been squeezed out, like the breath from a python's victim. My life was isolated and insular. Work was my only lifeline but eventually if that's all there is, even that takes more than it gives. Surely, there had to be more to life.

I am counted among those who go down to the pit; I am like one without strength. *Psalm 88:4*

Mark had always been strangely self-righteous about cigarette smoking: to him it was a hanging offence — the unforgivable sin. He smelled cigarette smoke on me one day when we were somewhere down the country. Swiftly and silently he got on his bike, revved it hard and began riding away. I had to jump on while he roared past, or be left behind. I was now free to smoke myself sick, but it was no consolation. I undertook the inevitable road trips to Kaitoke alone. Six hours there, six hours back, for a two-hour visit, if we were lucky. On one occasion visitors were kept waiting outside until there was only half an hour left. Codependency is a very hard taskmaster.

When Meg and Robbie came with me, we chain-smoked cigarettes and cannabis all the way down. We reeked. Mark smelt the stink on me from fifty paces, cursed loudly, and refused to visit at all.

Another time, I was tired from driving all night. The sunrise peeped over the hills, hinting at something better as I drove through a very windy part of the road. Clinging to the beauty on the horizon, I missed the sign indicating a 45kph warning for a hairpin bend ahead. I took the blind corner on the wrong side of the road. A flimsy old wire fence stopped me tumbling over the edge and dropping a couple hundred metres to the bottom.

Someone had been looking out for me. Again.

I will lead the blind by ways they have not known, along unfamiliar paths I will guide them; I will turn the darkness into light before them and make the rough places smooth. These are the things I will do; I will not forsake them. *Isaiah 42:16*

Still, for all my deadness, the ache inside persisted. The people and things I thought I wanted did nothing to fill the emptiness. I thought Mark would be the answer to my loneliness when he came back, but when he finally came home from jail his words did mortal damage to my desperate heart.

"I want to go home. I miss my family."

There are just no words to describe how I felt that Mark would rather have been in jail than with me. There was now nothing to hope for to stop the ache. There was nothing left I hadn't tried.

Mark slept on the floor in the tiny laundry because the open space was overwhelming. He gradually acclimatised and spent his days playing the 'Doom', day after day — week in, week out. Disappointment, hurt and hopelessness pressed in on every side and I was getting heartily sick of it by now. I was still on my own. But it was somehow worse.

Those moments between sleeping and waking were bliss. When it was possible that it was all just a nightmare that would ebb away when I woke. The first few seconds after I realised it wasn't a nightmare, I braced myself for the weight of responsibility and the dark cloud of despair which settled squarely on my shoulders like a halo. The spirit of death was romancing me. Sometimes I would walk to the end of South Street, look down on the motorway and wonder what it would be like to jump off the bridge. I wanted to, but I knew I didn't have the courage.

In the ancient Karangahape Road cemetery at Grafton I found a form of peace, or welcome deadness in the midst of chaos, sometimes guiltily lying down on top of someone's grave.

> But God will redeem me from the realm of the dead; he will surely take me to himself.
> *Psalm 49:15*

For a couple of years, Mum and Dad had practised Tough Love and ceased contact with me, trying to get the message through about Mark. I barely noticed, but they had to try.

"Janet, you've changed," Sam said one day. She'd lost one sibling and was worried she'd lose another.

"So?" I barked and shook my head.

I'd hated who I'd been before and was glad I'd changed. Good riddance to that faceless drone. I couldn't handle the truth. My life was wrong and downright ugly, but I couldn't fix it. From time to time, a momentary lapse of denial would confront, but I would quickly divert and carry on as though nothing had happened.

I lay on the dirty footpath on East Street with my mangy, stray street cat. It had some kind of horrible skin condition and wasn't very nice to touch. We were a good pair. My subconscious nudged again at how far I had fallen, and to wake up. Last night I'd been walking back down East Street from Karangahape Road in the dark by myself, which wasn't the safest thing to do. A bottom feeder materialised from the shadows and walked boldly in step with me, subliminally communicating I was about to be mugged.

"Don't even think about it!" I snarled, beast mode being my default mode these days. The creature of the night reeled back and the darkness received its own.

I was an emotional deadbeat with a go-getter mask, striving hard to keep things together. The cannabis was so strong I could literally hear my brain frying and making buzzing and popping noises. I sometimes wondered what I would do once my brain was completely f*@ked. I couldn't come up with an answer so would shrug the question off as lightly as if I just couldn't decide what to have for dinner. But slowly and surely I was starting to get sick of being a dope. So I quit. I gave up cannabis, and with that my security blanket was gone. My pain turned to anger. Something had to give.

"Stop playing that stupid game or f*@k off!" I shouted at Mark one day. He stopped. New 'friends' appeared from nowhere. Mark had money again, and he showed his love by giving gifts. I asked no questions and was told nothing for my own protection. We lived in parallel worlds. Little did I know, we would have been better off if Mark had just played Doom all day.

The pressure of keeping Paradox going had taken its toll. I was burnt out. There was either too much work, or none at all. Mark's money kept Paradox alive during the lean months, when natural selection dictated it should have died a natural death. It became hard to remain competitive as more and more corporates moved their printing offshore.

There was no place to turn to find relief. To me, rest and peace were simply theoretical constructs, luxuries others enjoyed. For many years my attempts to find restorative sleep at night were thwarted by nightmares and a disturbing, recurring 'screaming' issue. I'd suddenly sit bolt upright and scream and scream with all my might, totally unaware of what I was doing. One night Mark confronted me while it was happening.

"What the f*@k are you doing?"

I stopped and calmly answered him, "What do you mean?"

"You nearly gave me a f*@king heart attack! You just wake up and scream your head off sometimes for no reason."

The 'night terrors' were sometimes so bad that sometimes I'd wake up on the other side of the room, or at the bottom of the ladder to our loft bedroom with my arm half dislocated. I'd be very, very scared and sometimes hurt myself flying around the room or trying to climb the walls.

Psychology's take on night terrors, or sleep terrors, is that people experience a rude awakening, give a penetrating cry, sit bolt upright and stare blankly while suffering deep-seated panic and inexplicable over-stimulation of the autonomic nervous system. Few remember a coherent dream, but some retain an alarming image. The textbook goes on to say this is not indicative of emotional disturbance and treatment may not be required as night terrors are often temporary.

My night terrors were definitely not a temporary problem, and recollection of my 'dreams' was generally vivid and disturbing on much more than just an autonomic level. In my humble opinion, night terrors and the scary image usually recalled by sufferers is purely demonic, and would not be cured by any amount of psychological treatment, being highly indicative of emotional disturbance. Doors had been opened which should never have been opened. Doors had been opened which I couldn't close.

There was only one who could.

See darkness covers the earth and thick darkness is over the peoples, but the Lord rises upon you and his glory appears over you. Nations will come to your light, and kings to the brightness of your dawn.
Isaiah 60:2

ভ৯৹ ৯৹৹

Unable to sleep, I stared at the ceiling. Mark's even breathing told me he was out. He'd told me a few years before that I could have a baby if I wanted. That had never been something I'd thought about at all, and certainly had never seen myself as a mother. But Sam had been talking about it, and thought I may as well catch this boat with her.

"Well, if you have one, I'll have one" I said coldly.

Now the time had come, I had changed my mind. I wasn't ready. Nevertheless, a nagging feeling told me it was happening, ready or not. I climbed down the ladder and padded to the bathroom to undertake The Test. It was as I feared. I sat on the toilet, numbly staring at the positive result for a full ten minutes, as if staring at it long enough it would change it to negative.

However, the only thing that was to change was life as I knew it.

> I will pour out my Spirit on your offspring, and my blessing on your descendants. *Isaiah 44:3*

Mark grunted and rolled over when I shared the happy news, although I should have waited until he was conscious I suppose.

Pete was concerned. "How are you going to cope?"

"Nothing's going to change around here," I confidently assured him. I had no idea that only a few short weeks after Roq was born, Paradox would close for good.

One of Mark's friends dropped in for a visit and I blurted out the big news and followed it up a few seconds later with uncontrollable crying, tears squirting out of my eyes, snot cascading from my nose like a 3D version of Spongebob Squarepants. He stared at me, eyes bugging, mind whirling. A class act. I'd given up smoking cannabis for the sake of the baby, but as hormones raged I lost the battle for control. Lying in the fetal position on the couch, weeping hysterically I tried unsuccessfully to pull myself together for hours and hours.

"Oh for goodness sake, have a smoke," Mark said finally, unable to take any more. "At least it will calm you down." It did. The cigarettes helped too. I was very calm after that.

> My frame was not hidden from you when I was made in the secret place, when I was woven together in the depths of the earth. Your eyes saw my unformed body; all the days ordained for me were written in your book before one of them came to be.
> *Psalm 139:15-16*

⁙

Our lives were a paradox. While we worked, more often than not the office hosted hard core Westie marathons all hours of the day and night. I worked as though my life depended on it, regardless of what was happening at the table in the middle of the office, and stayed straight for six years, not counting cannabis. People accepted that I didn't drink; they'd never seen me as a drinker. But I'd given up the meth, then cannabis (until I got pregnant) and it had made people uncomfortable. I'd gone straight. I might as well have got religion. The joke was, "Hey Janet, do you still do coffee?"

One morning I cleared the mess, ignoring miscellaneous sleeping people before I started work. I'd kept my end of the rehab bargain but Mark hadn't kept his. It was party central. Eventually, I finished up the day's work, and headed off to bed with no dinner. I wasn't cooking for that lot. A new guy had crawled off to a couch earlier in the afternoon and was sleeping it off, still sitting up. The party at Paradox continued through the night.

The next morning I was grumpy. I came down the ladder and was confronted by ambulance officers carrying the new guy out on a stretcher. His lungs had filled with fluid over the hours he'd sat in a drug-induced coma. Mark was all damage control. If he'd given up meth, this wouldn't have happened. I was angry he hadn't kept his word. I hated my life. I hated my guilt. I hated myself. My life was one big ugly mess. I just didn't have what it took to walk away and leave my partner, work, clients, and home all at once.

Someone had to do it for me.

> O paradox of heaven.
> The load we think will crush us
> was sent to lift us up to God!
> Then, soul of mine, climb up!
> Nothing can e'er be crushed
> save what is underneath the weight.
>
> How may we climb!
> By what ascent will we crest
> the critical cares of life!
> Within his word is found the key
> which opens his secret stairs;
> Alone with Christ, secluded there,
> we mount our loads, and rest in him.

Streams in the Desert, Mary Butterfield, March 9

9. Déjà vu

1999
Voices drifted to meet me as I lay on the couch suffering a mother of a migraine headache. The morning traffic was bringing spaghetti junction to life just outside the window. The cool, wet towel soothed my brow. The spew bucket vied for space on my lap with my pregnant tummy and needed emptying.

I'd met our unborn baby last night. The baby I had successfully denied had introduced himself. The one I'd ignored for six months was tired of being ignored. While I slept, my baby's face appeared before my eyes. His big blue eyes danced with mine. Squeals of joy punctuated the belly laugh and touched my heart. Roq Robert Balcombe was real.

You created my inmost being; you knit me together in my mother's womb. *Psalm 139:13*

It was 5.59 a.m. The joyous laugh still resonated in my spirit, confronting my pain. How long had it been since I had really laughed? Since I had been happy? I was challenged to take a good hard look at my life, but once again it was too hard.

The whole idea of motherhood had triggered a paradigm shift. Respect for my mother and what she went through. Respect for the mother of Mark's kids, and respect for them. They were great kids. Their acceptance broke my heart. They should hate me. Josh was a teenager and had lived with us at Symonds Street. I had confronted Mark about involving Josh in the 'business.' I couldn't stomach sitting by and watching Josh being led off down the well-travelled road to nowhere. Thankfully the message seemed to get through, and the apprenticeship had been aborted.

Danielle was very young when from time to time she came and stayed with us at Paradox. I didn't like kids, but Danielle was different. She ate lemons. She helped me deliver the print jobs sometimes. We rode the elevator up to the top of the Stock Exchange tower together and laughed as our tummies went whoop. She brought a new perspective. I never had to worry about her. She always behaved. While I spoke with the guys, she would make her way quietly to the window, put her head against the glass and marvel at the little people scurrying along Queen Street.

Danielle was often heart-broken, waiting in vain for Mark's visit on birthdays and at other times. Mark would want to go but refused to go without me. I was stuck in no-man's-land, wanting to go to please a little girl and her father but unable to endure the wrath of her mother's girlfriends again. Eventually, they moved to Australia so they couldn't be hurt anymore.

The ache in my soul was deep. I'd broken up a family. I'd taken their Dad away. This was the root of my guilt and above all else, what I hated most about my life. I'd fallen in love with Mark before I'd found out he was married with children. It didn't matter that I'd turned him down every day for two weeks before finally going out with him, or that if I'd known he was married it would never have happened at all. What mattered was that when I did have the facts, I didn't walk away. It was like a car crash. It was irrelevant who was at fault. There's just such a bloody mess: in the end it doesn't even matter.

I will repay you for the years the locusts have eaten.
Joel 2:25

"I met our baby last night," I had told Mark, "in a dream."

"Yea?" Mark said. The second-hand information didn't convey the beauty and joy of my encounter.

I moved the damp cloth to find another cool spot. Had I known that the front door of Paradox was silently crawling with black wasps from the Auckland Drug Squad I'd really have had something to get a migraine over. Ours was not the only door swarming at that moment for this operation. Mark and the guys were still in the boardroom, digging deep into their ounces of meth, smoking joints and sinking beers.

The clock ticked over to 6 a.m. The drug squad crashed the front door. *"STAY WHERE YOU ARE! DON'T MOVE!"*

Here we go again. The guys had stashed their bags in the second before the drug squad poured into the room.

"NO TALKING! KEEP YOUR HANDS WHERE I CAN SEE THEM! DON'T MOVE!"

Another search warrant flashed, 'conspiring to manufacture methamphetamine'. Cops kept their eyes fixed upon us; others ransacked. Every drawer, cupboard and room was turned upside down in pursuit of incriminating evidence.

I was strip-searched by a woman detective, and denied my breakfast because the pantry had to be searched first. Not the way to start the day. I was getting annoyed.

"Sit at the table and don't move," my detective said. He sat with me to make sure I didn't pull anything smart. Mark and the others were separated, searched and watched in another room. Time passed slowly as the police went about their business. This wasn't good. I had work to do. I had just secured a new client, the corporate banking department of a major bank. Their first project lay partially completed on my desk, and today was the day I had to deliver a mock-up of their new corporate presentation folder for approval. Today, it seemed, was the day for many things.

The phone rang. My detective pounced.

"It's for you," he said, holding the phone to me.

"Oh, it's not for you? Take a message."

"You'd better take it. It's #$&@!" he said, a little freaked out by who was calling. *(The name has been protected, this is not a cuss word.)*

"Tell them I'm not here!"

"Come on! It's #$&@!" He was panicking, and I felt a little sorry for him. I snatched the phone.

"Hello, Janet speaking."

"Good morning Janet. William was wondering what time he can expect the presentation folder today?" asked the personal assistant.

"Right. At this point, I'm not sure of the exact time, but as soon as I know, I'll give you a bell and let you know."

"That would be wonderful. William is looking forward to seeing it."

"That's great. Thanks for the call."

I watched as the cops walked out the door with the crucial computer that housed the job. This was not good. In fact, I almost lost my faculties once and for all.

"How long before I get the computer back?" I asked my detective.

"A few weeks, a few months, if at all."

"I need it back right away," I said firmly, fully aware of the absurdity of my request.

Mark emerged from the boardroom and threw the customary goodbye glance over his shoulder as he was, once again, marched away in handcuffs. My mind raced forward to a codependent new mother's worst nightmare: giving birth to her baby without the father present. I decided there and then, if Mark didn't make it to the delivery suite for whatever reason, he might as well not come home at all. Jail wasn't a valid excuse.

The phone rang again. My cop pounced. "It's for you," he said.

"Take a message!" I was sick of him now.

"It's your father," he said with 'that look'.

"Hi."

"Hello. Your mother and I are just coming over the bridge now. We are going to Lucy's for our facials. We'll call in on the way back," Dad said.

I stared numbly. They lived two hours away, and they were just coming over the Auckland Harbour Bridge now? And they were going to call in later? Today couldn't be more demented had it been scripted by J. J. Abrams. What could possibly happen next? Absolutely anything, so it seemed.

Lucy, the girlfriend of Mark's new 'buddy', ran a beauty salon out of her home. I received facials, products and gift vouchers in return for designing and printing her stationery. Mum and Dad were the proud recipients of facial vouchers for Christmas. And they chose today to redeem them.

"Um, I'm not feeling well — migraine." True, although that was the least of my problems now. "It might be better if you didn't."

Silence. Traffic noise. The sound of cops methodically trashing our place.

"Hmm, ok. Well, we'll call in anyway. See you later." Dad smelled a rat.

"Ok," I said, feeling sicker by the minute. Hopefully I'd be in jail by then. The cop and I sat staring at each other for a while. Well, he stared. I glared. Work was pressing.

"Sorry, I'd love to sit here all day, but I've got work to do," I said, taking a seat at the desk. The detective watched in disbelief as I put in a call to the die-cutters. Breaking all the rules, I carried on with the project. Having no computer was just not an option. I was not going to have a repeat of the last debacle. That was getting old. This job was going to get done come hell or high water, or both.

"Good morning, it's Janet from Paradox. I'm ringing about the die-line for the #$&@ folder."

I organised the cutting-form for the folder and booked the job in under the watchful eye of my new best friend. His eyes told the story. Understanding. Respect. It was a paradox indeed that this bunch of outlaws had such an interesting set of clients, and such an iron-clad work ethic. I hung up the phone, deep in thought.

"Where did you learn that?" he asked.

"Here, at Paradox," I replied. "We do real work here. I need the computer back today." I probably had a better chance of winning an Academy Award for Best Actress, but I had to ask. The detective was a good guy. In fact, he seemed genuinely concerned about the bank.

"I'll see what I can do. No promises," he said quietly.

ംൊ൦ ൦ൊം

Across town, Mum and Dad pulled up outside Lucy's house. They noticed the team of people in white overalls swarming over the property. Some carried bulging black sacks. Some carried clipboards. Some carried torches and ladders. The inconvenient truth was dawning on the olds.

They trudged up the path with heavy hearts. Dad heard the sergeant speak to the detective.

"This might be The Boss," said the Sergeant, eyeing Dad's white Mercedes.

"Who are you here to see?" he asked.

'We have an appointment with Lucy for facials," Dad said.

"Oh, Lucy won't be doing any facials today," he said, smirking. "Who are you? Where are you from?"

"Ray and Bev from Ruawai," said Dad, cringing.

"Right," said the cop, scrutinising him carefully with one eye and making notes with the other.

"We'll be on our way then," Dad suggested hopefully.

"Right," said the detective, noting the number plate. Dad took Mum by the elbow and steered her back up the path. Then he made the call to me.

"Hello?"

"Hello." I braced myself. "Your mother and I have decided not to call in today. We'll catch up with you another time." Dad thought for a moment about mentioning that Lucy's place was being busted, then decided against it. Just as well.

Despite Dad's efforts to avoid being in the wrong place at the wrong time, they still had been. They travelled home in silence, the question hanging between them, "My God, can it get any worse?"

And the answer remained, yes, it could.

Incredibly, the cop moved heaven and earth and the computer returned that afternoon once the hard drive had been mirrored. I met with the bank later that same day, seemingly composed and professional, and dying on the inside. Returning to our home and office, I picked my way through the rubble of our lives to the couch.

I sat with my unborn baby and wept.

I will pour water on the thirsty land, and streams on the dry ground. *Isaiah 44:3*

Eventually, Mark returned home to begin another lag of bail conditions while the police built their case. We prepared to move out of East Street into an old suburban home in Mount Roskill with Josh.

Ordinarily the last few weeks of pregnancy are no picnic. I'd been scrubbing the filthy, dark Mount Roskill kitchen. My mood matched my surrounds. The angry wrinkles chiselled between my brows were now a permanent feature. Even when I did smile, the smile never reached my eyes anymore. When I was ready to leave, I discovered that Mark had already left for East Street to do another load. He'd been going back and forth all morning, but he just happened to be 'forth', not 'back' at the precise moment I needed him. I could have had a rest. But no, that trivial fact triggered an avalanche that buried me under everything I hated about my life. I started walking. It began to rain. Mark discovered me on the footpath halfway to the inner city and did his best to encourage me into the car. I hurled abuse at him and continued walking the six kilometres in silent fury to East Street.

My baby decided he'd had enough. He wanted out. Not long after that, Roq Robert Balcombe made his entrance into the world, three weeks early. He was small, 6lb 4oz and very, very perfect. The nurse tossed him up onto my chest and those familiar big, clear blue eyes studied me. He looked right into my soul. Without words, he said to me, "So you're it."

"So you're it," I replied.

> You will go out in joy and be led forth in peace; the mountains and hills will burst into song before you, and all the trees of the field will clap their hands. Instead of the thornbush will grow the juniper, and instead of briers the myrtle will grow. This will be for the Lord's renown, for an everlasting sign, that will endure forever.
> *Isaiah 55:12-13*

The next day brought Mark to visit his new son. He was proud. He'd been with me when Roq was born, for which I was very grateful. We looked into the face of the miracle baby who arrived after we had been together for a decade, and survived against the odds. Out of nowhere my heart was overcome with guilt for having smoked cannabis throughout my pregnancy. I didn't deserve the baby. Overwhelmed with grief, I wept and wailed loudly.

Cannabis was the hardest drug for me to quit, hands down. To bottle-feed seemed the only decent option, as I was still smoking.

Things were about to get interesting. We brought Roq home from the hospital to his new world. As I had thought ante-natal classes were for wimps, I simply didn't know what to do with him. I put him on a huge mountain of washing. He wanted milk, and I didn't know how to make a bottle. I hadn't prepared a nursery for him. He had no place of his own. Baby clothes and gifts people had given us were scattered about the place. You could say I was unprepared. Meeting Roq in the dream had made room in my heart for him, but I had no head-space for baby prep whatsoever. Keeping the clients happy and moving house in my last trimester took everything I had, and more. Having never been around people with babies, they were a foreign species, and I was a stranger in their land.

A car door closed outside. Super Mum had arrived. It was May, a mother of six children and a wealth of experience that money can't buy. She was understandably shocked at the state of us. She rolled her sleeves up and got to work, choosing an area in our room for Roq. She set up a changing table, and a basket for him to sleep in. She folded and sorted his clothes, and stacked them on shelves. She showed me how to feed, change, bath and burp. She returned with a friend and cleaned. May and her husband O'Neill took Roq some weekends to give me a breather.

This is what angels look like.

The cheery, motherly Plunket Nurse paid a visit.

"Oh, yes, he's beautiful," she reported, "and you're doing a wonderful job. I love his name: Roq. He's not a pebble, he's a beautiful Ayers' Rock (Uluru)," she trilled in her melodious manner. Her mood sobered. She seemed to be listening to something I couldn't hear. "Even at three months, I can tell if you don't get control of him, there'll be trouble. He's very strong-willed."

She was right. It was game on. Pete's words rang in my ears, "How are you going to cope, Janet?" My wise friend must have had a premonition.

"Nothing's going to change around here," I had trumpeted confidently. Joke.

Before long, I was at the point of exhaustion. Roq was having the worst colic and constipation known to baby man. How could a baby cry so much without doing himself a mischief? Fear of cot death, and of doing something wrong haunted me, so I checked on him relentlessly. He cried most of the time, and barely slept. Combine severe sleep deprivation with no day-to-day help, and I was in bad shape.

One morning I awoke to the screaming baby. Something was wrong with my eyes. They were the opposite of cross-eyed, had parted company, and were literally going in different directions. I sat on the side of the bed and tried for a minute or two to pull them back into alignment. It wasn't working, and panic was rising. I was sure I would never recover. Eventually, I reigned them back in by sheer willpower. I was in trouble.

But those who hope in the Lord will renew their strength. They will soar on wings like eagles; they will run and not grow weary, they will walk and not be faint. *Isaiah 40:31*

✦✦✦

The investment bank rang.

"Janet, I'm sorry, we're going to be taking our printing offshore now, like the rest of our branches. Everyone's doing it now."

"Wow. Ok."

"But we still want you to do our design."

"Sorry, no printing, no Paradox."

After a couple of months trying to tie up loose ends, Paradox closed down for good. It was the end of an era. Unbeknown to us, our accountant was an accident waiting to happen. A couple of years earlier, we had him change the business status from partnership to a limited company, or so we thought. The only thing was, now there were two companies, a partnership, and a limited company. You'd think he would have noticed.

The dual sets of tax and GST bills we continually received were telling, for starters, and they just didn't stop coming. No matter how much I complained, he just couldn't seem to put it right. We paid him good money, but that didn't make him any better at his job. He was a lemon. We had always paid our bills. I rang the tax department and tried to sort it out myself, time and time again. I repeated myself until I was blue in the face, but no matter what I did, the postman delivered new sets of GST bills demanding a feral amount of money which continued to grow larger and more ferociously than a cancerous tumour.

Originally, everything to do with the business had been put under my name for obvious reasons. I was now personally receiving tax bills totalling $26,000, and counting. This vampire was sucking the life out of me. It just wouldn't die. I came to a perfect understanding of how people end up topping themselves from this sort of financial pressure. To survive, I stopped opening the bills, instead blankly tossing them onto a burgeoning pile in a shoebox. I rolled over and played dead. No matter what I did, I was pushing crap uphill with a rake. I became more bitter and cynical by the day.

There was a knock at the door. I answered with Roq on my hip. It was Max. I was less than overjoyed to see him. I'd had it with Mark's mates. This lifestyle didn't seem to be doing much for us.

"Is Mark here?" he asked. I gave him a filthy look and turned away, leaving him at the door. He came in and found Mark.

"Check my wagon, bro!" I heard him say.

I looked out the window. It was riddled with fresh bullet holes from one of the larger west Auckland gangs. And he comes here, thanks very much. My narrator was off on a rant that didn't stop until I almost became completely unhinged. Mark found it highly entertaining, of course, most excellent value, and he wanted all the gory details.

"I was at home by myself, I was cleaning my gun at the time, and I saw them coming! There were five of them. They were coming to take my boat. I hid behind the boat and started shooting. They shot at me too. I got a couple of them in the legs, the others ran away."

It was just another day at the office in the wild west. They kept talking, but I'd heard enough. When Max had gone, Mark came to see me. "Max wants us to move into this cool place in Titirangi. It's got million dollar views, and it's really cheap. We can move now. Let's go have a look, eh?"

"Ok," I said, knowing it wasn't the smartest choice in the world, but thoroughly sick of the dark, damp and dirty Mount Roskill house. So we did. We had little income, received no government support, and things were starting to unravel very fast. I was losing my grip.

It was a mansion nestled in the bush at the end of a long winding driveway on Park Road. It was stunning, with views of native bush, Auckland city, and Rangitoto Island. There were large holes smashed into walls for dodgy drug business, and it was on the market but never mind about that. The place was incredible.

We moved in with Max and Josh. Another new 'mate' materialised, and soon after their mysterious activities were stalked discreetly by police helicopters, bugs, and most other forms of surveillance. Mark's theory: if he was going down for conspiring to manufacture methamphetamine, he might as well do it and make some money before he went to jail.

One clear and starry night, Mark and I stood in the games room in the dark, looking out at the gorgeous view.

"See that house over there?" he said to me quietly, pointing to a house across the valley. I could see a couple of silhouettes standing at the large window.

"Yep."

"They're watching us."

Instantly they disappeared, and the lights went out. We were living inside a ticking time bomb. When panic rose, I pushed it down. I didn't think I could cope with another move so soon, and goodness knows what would happen to Mark. I guess you're not paranoid if they really are after you. A certain law of physics seemed to be at work. Everything was sliding downhill at an exponential rate, especially my moral and cognitive state. Mark warned me not to come to the P-lab under any circumstances, but I took Roq where angels fear to tread. The smell of chemicals was indescribable. I was aware the whole place could have gone up with no provocation at all, but it didn't register. The lights were on, but I had officially left the building. Again.

History repeats, and shortly after, we were served a Notice of Eviction and had three days to get out. With no time or money to find a place big enough to house all Mark's furniture and toys, we put everything into storage while we carried on looking. Trouble was, we didn't find a place for nearly three months. Everywhere was too expensive, or too small. Roq was six months old and lived in his car seat most of the time. Eventually, he couldn't stand to be put into his car seat anymore. We did the washing and sterilised bottles at mates' places when we called in to visit, or stay a night.

The anguish of moving out of the house when we had nowhere else to go was intense. I'd fallen out of Maslow's box again, but this time I had a babe in my arms.

A West Auckland motel was home for a couple of days. I woke up and went to make Roq his bottle only to find there was no power. I popped Roq in the pram to take him for a walk and kill some time until the power came back on. On the street only a hundred yards or so from the motel, we came across a fatal accident. Van versus power-pole. Police and rescue worked hard to free the driver from the wreck. We watched the ambulance depart and the tow-truck drive away with the wrecked van. I went back to the unit and found Mark awake. As I described the van, his face went pale. He'd been expecting a mate. The mate was late, and that was why.

"Well, that's that!" Mark said, shocked and angry. I thought for a moment he was upset about his friend. "The towies would have got my hundred grand, and the guns I need for a meeting today with one of the gangs that's looking *very dodgy*. And he had the raw material for the next cook."

He had said it before and he said it again; "People die around me."

The spirit of death blew its cover all the time. Sometimes it worked suddenly, on other victims the python slowly tightened its grip, day by day. Each time its victim breathed out, the python tightened its grip a little more until it just couldn't take another breath. Like with me, for example.

This was way too much. Grief for the life lost and tragic waste overwhelmed me. No one cared about the mate. I'd only met him a couple of times, and didn't understand why I couldn't stop crying. When we attended the funeral, I cried and cried. I cried so much that people suspected I must have been having an affair with the guy. I continued crying well after the funeral. I cried for a couple of days.

I shall turn their hearts of stone into hearts of flesh.
Ezekiel 36:26

At the wake, I watched in disbelief as Mark and some mates methodically searched the grounds of their mate's home in plain sight for some gear they believed was buried there, blind to the large group of mourners nearby. It was like a bad trip. A hallucination. This just couldn't be happening. I was sickened and embarrassed. I wanted then, more than at any other time to leave, but still just couldn't see the door.

Our money had run out, so once again we packed our gear into the Terrano and headed off down the highway to hell in top gear. The frustration of a mother with no home in which to care for her baby was torturous. Only Roq kept me going. At least we have the wagon, I thought. Wait, what was that noise? The engine was making a weird noise and the temperature gauge was in the red.

"Look at it! It's got no oil! The motor is blowing!" Mark shrieked hysterically. I contained the urge to slap his face hard.

"Well stop!" I shouted.

"Listen to it!" he screamed like a lunatic and put his foot down it until it finally blew up. Just when we thought we had nothing left, we lost more. I hated him then. Why did he have to do that? What was that?

"It's f*@ked," he said unnecessarily. Any moron could see that.

He got out, slammed the door and stalked off down the road. Tears streamed down my face, and Roq screamed, captive in his car seat. I screamed, captive in my life.

But God will never forget the needy; the hope of the afflicted will never perish. *Psalm 9:18*

---

10. Rock bottom

2001

"It's a little flat in Waitakere, pretty small, but at least it's somewhere," I said to Mark.

"Well, it'll be better than sleeping in the wagon."

It wasn't big enough for all our gear so we kept a lock-up and moved what fit into a small, two-bedroom flat on the outskirts of west Auckland. Chickens ranged freely through our house from the neighbouring farm when the doors were open. Roq loved it, and so did I, until the chooks pooped everywhere. The first day, I went to the neighbours, introduced myself, and asked to borrow some food for our dinner. They were decent people and gave us a meal and a dozen eggs. The bliss of having our own shower and toilet, our own kitchen and floor for Roq to stretch out on was wonderful. We finally had somewhere to be.

Roq had always suffered from colic and constipation and was often screaming in pain, and I never really knew why he was crying. He was taking a little solid food now but still suffered terrible colic until he eventually stopped having formula. It was a real struggle for us all, not least of all for Roq.

Mark got a job working with the landlord at the local garbage dump. It wasn't much, but it was a real job, and I was proud of him for taking it. But as time went on, he became more and more depressed by life in general, the only blip on the horizon being the prospect of jail. His bail conditions were very tough to keep now that we lived thirty kilometres away from the police station, and the wagon was still out of action. We were stuck out in the wilderness with no wheels.

Roq was finally sleeping peacefully. I tucked the beautiful little man into his cot and looked forward to having a rest. I lay down on the bed and closed my eyes, only to awake moments later to an incredible noise from Roq's room. I leapt up and saw Mark leaning over the cot screaming full noise into Roq's face.

"WAKE UP, YOU F*@CKING ASSHOLE! WHY SHOULD YOU SLEEP WHEN I NEVER CAN BECAUSE OF YOU? WAKE UP!"

Roq was about as scared as someone can get, and screamed his head off. I snatched him up and took him into our room. He was badly shaken. Clutching him tightly, we both wept bitterly. We listened and cried as Mark trashed everything that belonged to Roq. His wooden cot, highchair, car seat, bouncer and walker; everything was smashed to pieces and thrown out onto the lawn in a heap. This was a special kind of crazy. My pain was beyond agony. We had just taken one step forward and twenty back. The root of fear shot down deep into Roq's heart, and it would be over a decade before he could overcome it. And something else died that day. Something big.

Time ticked on, and Mark's court case was fast approaching. He seemed more intent on getting tattoos than on getting his case sorted with his lawyer. It was inevitable that jail was coming, and tattoos were the best thing to help him in there. They were mana. The more you had, the more you were respected and left alone. It mattered not that there was little space for many more.

Roq and I took the train into town for a ride with Mark sometimes when he checked in, for a fun, family outing, but even this was a struggle. There was very little time in which to check in at Auckland Central then haul ass back up to the Mount Eden train station in time to catch the last train back home. There was no margin for error, and we ran full tilt, with Roq in the pram to make it in time. Roq hung on for dear life with all his might, to not be thrown out. I found him when we finally arrived at the station once, sitting up in his pram, sound asleep still with his little hands in an iron grip on the front bar of his pram.

Roq still cried a lot. He was insecure and scared, especially of Mark. We had no routine. With so many moves in such a short time and our stuff all over the place, I couldn't get my act together easily. Roq knew the ones who were charged with his care were out of control, and he was right. So was the Plunket Nurse. Survival instinct is an incredible thing. Mine worked against us, clinging onto the devil I knew with all my might. But at ten months of age, Roq had already subconsciously decided if he was going to get through this, he was going to have to be The Boss.

I had been off P for two years, but was still very thin and utterly exhausted. I was miserable deep down, but wouldn't let myself dwell on that. The problems were too great to begin to sort out, so every time I bumped into them it was still best to carry on as if nothing had happened. Mum and Dad visited occasionally now which was nice for me, not so nice for them. Dad shared his concern that he'd been worried I would kill myself.

"Dad, if I was going to do that, I'd have done it ages ago." I replied. "I wanted to, but I couldn't."

Letters and cards arrived sometimes from Mum containing lots of love and usually a scripture from the Bible. It sounds inoffensive enough, but I found the scriptures absolutely maddening. They triggered a spiritual reaction and a tirade of cuss words. They always left me with the question, "Why does she have to do that?" as if she was the one with the problem.

❦❦

Things hadn't gone well. There had been a standoff with one of the gangs Mark cooked meth for. Mark warned me to 'expect a visit'. He said they usually kill the women and kids, kidnap the meth cook and make him work for free until they were done with him, then killed him too. He slept with a loaded gun under his pillow, but was actually so low he didn't care anymore if they killed him. Or us. I questioned Mark's casual sacrifice of Roq and me for money.

"So it's ok with you that you're putting our lives at risk?"

"It's just the price we pay," he said gallantly.

Mark's mates soon arrived and they began hatching a new plan. I looked at him in disbelief as he sat talking with the guys about another cook. I'd had enough. When the guys had gone I issued an ultimatum. Stop the cooking or I'm leaving with Roq. Of course he didn't believe I actually would. Or could. Neither did I, but it would be better to die trying than die like a sitting duck. The warning went unheeded, and as expected, I couldn't leave. So there was a divine intervention.

Roq was a year old now, thriving in the bliss of having room to play and sleep. He was getting around, into everything, just being Snoopy. He toddled in from outside one day with chicken poop smeared around his mouth.

"Mmm," I said, "yummy."

He gave me a two-tooth grin and a squeal. A couple of days later it wasn't so cute. Roq had severe vomiting and diarrhoea at the same time, and was unable to keep anything down at all, not even water. As soon as I changed his nappy, he moved, and it needed changing again. I loaded him into the wagon and drove him to the doctor, fighting nausea and fever myself.

"Campylobacter. Bacterial food poisoning," the doctor said after we had gone through the painstaking process of delivering two fresh faecal samples to the lab from somewhere way out past the edge.

"It usually takes a couple of weeks for the stomach pains, vomiting and diarrhoea to pass. Just try to keep some fluid in him," came the diagnosis. "Yea, good luck with that," my narrator muttered.

Eventually Roq started to get better, but now I had a full-blown case myself. I couldn't keep water down. I had already been in pretty bad condition to begin with. Another week or more of trying to care for Roq and myself was just too much. It took a supernatural effort just to make a bottle or change him. Mark was in a pit of black depression. He knew jail was getting closer every day and couldn't see past the end of his nose. He had given up work by now and went about like a zombie, stepping over me as I lay on the floor in the lounge close enough to the toilet that I could drag myself.

I had reached the end of the road. I was physically unable to go another day.

The feeling of swimming against the tide was now a feeling of drowning in the dead marshes. I barely had the energy, or will, to raise a hand for help. I lay in silent wonder at Mark's lack of compassion for Roq and me. A question welled up in my soul.

"Why don't you help us?" I asked Mark.

"Why don't you go to your parents?" As was his habit, he answered my question with another question. Right. What choice did I have? If it hadn't been for Roq, I wouldn't have bothered and probably just would have died of organ failure. After fighting for so many years, I knew I'd finally hit the bottom of the pit. With the last remaining dollar of credit on my cell, I phoned home, hoping desperately it wouldn't be wasted on an answering machine.

"Hello?" said Dad. Relief flooded in, and I breathed again.

"Hi. Can you come and get Roq and me please? We're not very well."

"Ok, just pack your bag, and I'll be there in a couple of hours," he said simply.

Wow. It was that easy. Wait, pack my bag? I wasn't able to do that. But I didn't want to be found by my father lying on the dirty floor in a dirty dressing gown, so I marshalled my strength and dragged myself up onto the couch. Roq sat quietly on the kitchen floor, bottle in hand, waiting for someone to come and fill it with milk. He waited. And waited.

Dad's tires eventually crunched to a stop in the driveway. Pop was greeted by a baby salute from Roq with his bottle. Pop took the hint and filled it with formula and made us a cup of tea. A little strength returned with the tea and compassion.

"Dad, I don't think I can pack our bags."

"You don't need much, just a few things."

We got it done. I said goodbye to Mark. "See you in a couple of days when I'm better," not realising how ill I was. Dad packed Roq and me into the car and we were off to Ruawai.

I didn't know I was leaving for good.

I lift up my eyes to the hills. From where does my help come? My help comes from the Lord, who made heaven and earth. He will not let your foot be moved; he who keeps you will not slumber.
Psalm 121:1-3

Back in Ruawai I walked like a toddler learning to walk, leaning on the furniture to get around. This was the second time Mum wished she had taken a photo, but hadn't. I propped myself up on the bench in the bathroom and looked into the mirror for the first time in a long time. I saw the mask of death. I was very shocked. I was seeing in the spirit, and a full-on skull was looking back at me. A skull that had white skin pulled tightly over its bones and dark, sunken eyes. I looked like a refugee from the zombie apocalypse.

I slept through the first couple of days but they made no dent in my recovery process. Had I really said I'd be back in a couple of days? As the weeks passed and my physical strength slowly grew, my mind began working again. The distance (and prayers of Mum and Mary) enabled me to see things from a different perspective. How they really were. And they were bad. But I was out. Why would I go back? I was only getting one shot at this life and I was blowing it. To be fair to Roq and myself, I couldn't go back, but I knew I didn't have the strength of will to stay away. I knew if I did go back I would somehow die, and Roq would repeat his father's footsteps. We would both be lost forever. And forever is a very long time.

Internally I started the process of leaving Mark. As I lay on the couch in the lounge, grief engulfed me and completely overwhelmed, leaving hardly a will to live. Struggling for breath, I had a thought.

"God, if you're real, you'd better show up now. I can't believe in something that's not real to me. There has to be more to it than words on a page. I can't do this on my own."

I waited and watched. No dramatic appearance of God or angelic presence in the room. It was just as I suspected. Nothing. Nada. Zilch. Despairing and broken, I released all hope, fearing greatly for our futures. If there was no real God, then who could help us? Mum and Dad could help with the necessaries of life, but who could fix my heart and restore to me once again, a will to live? I knew full well, left to my own devices I would go back. There were forces at work that bound me to him. Ties I couldn't break that worked constantly. Soul ties. I would, without doubt, spend my remaining time on this good earth going around in circles, repeating the same old mistakes and probably throwing in some new ones for good measure, dragging Roq behind me. I would go back to Mark, and that would be it. For both of us.

I lay at my lowest ebb on the tide of utter despair. Waves of excruciating hopelessness washed over and over me. I went through the following three days on automatic; numb and dead.

But God was at work.

I am making a way in the desert and streams in the wasteland. *Isaiah 43:19*

᠃ᠻ᠃

I went to bed and slept. In my dream, I opened the door and saw it. Like a scene straight out of The Exorcist, the Portacot was fully levitating in the air like a ship without the sea. The sides were breathing in and out like a macabre horror movie prop. And, well, you know the rest. If you didn't read the Prologue, go read it now.

I didn't know that God had heard my cry for help. He'd known all my life this day would come. However, his timing is not our timing. He is God, and we are not.

But if from there you seek the Lord your God, you will find him if you seek him with all your heart and with all your soul. *Deuteronomy 4:29*

God had pulled back the spiritual curtain and showed me the ugly truth in high definition 3D with surround sound. It was so bad I couldn't do my usual; brush myself off and pretend it didn't happen. There would be none of that this time. After Mum left for work I knew I had to go into that room and get the cot out. I didn't want Roq sleeping in there. Not after that. While Roq was in his highchair treating himself to a chocolate yoghurt facial, I steeled myself and entered the cold room. Fear chasing hard, hair standing on end, I was so freaked out I couldn't collapse the cot properly to get it through the door and nearly smashed it trying to ram it through the doorway, while still half up.

Mum's words ran through my mind all day.

"You can come to the prayer meeting tonight, if you want to."

Ah, NO! The very idea of going to a frickin' prayer meeting tonight was causing as much terror as going into the Exorcist room. That was the last thing I wanted to do. In fact, I didn't think I could go if my life depended on it. Only trouble was, it did. And deep down, I knew it.

"It's ok, you can just say you don't want to go, at the last minute," I told myself, over and over. "Yea, that's what I'll do," I was answering myself as well.

After dinner, it was time to go. There was a terrible battle happening in my spirit and in the spiritual realm. I knew I had to go, but with all my heart, I didn't want to. I felt like I'd rather die. I started crying. I knew I would cry but didn't think it'd start before I even left home. I had a total meltdown and couldn't pull myself together enough for us to leave. Mum prayed, and after that I was able to get into the car with her.

We pulled up at Mary's house, the Mary who'd prayed for me all those years. There seemed to be so many cars and that added to my panic. I walked into a room full of people, through a waterfall of tears. I was so scared. After a while, I realised that these religious ones were only people. They were kind, and we even had a few laughs. They began to sing. I was embarrassed. This was out of the realm of my experience and it wasn't my scene at all, but when they sang a song called, "Be still and know that I am God," I started to cry again.

They prayed and talked a bit and asked me what had been going on in my life. I stared into the comforting fire on that cold winter's night and told them some horror stories, doing my best to shock them, but they didn't seem shocked. An older gentleman named Merv Dodd spoke.

"Would you like us to pray for you?"

"Ok," I said.

He pulled a chair for me into the centre of the room so they could all stand around. It was weird. A young pastor in a leather jacket, Erin Underwood, asked if I wanted to accept Jesus into my heart to be my Lord and Saviour. I didn't know what that meant, but I thought I might as well, since he was asking. They prayed. I asked Jesus to live in my heart and be my Lord, and for me to be filled with the Holy Spirit. Mary said she could see Jesus holding a little lamb and smiling, and I was the lamb. Someone else said they could see God smiling in heaven.

It was July 24, 2001. I had finally come home to Jesus, the white light I'd always been so fascinated by.

Jesus answered, "I am the way, the truth and the life. No one comes to the Father except through me." *John 14:6*

Salvation is found in no one else, for there is no other name under heaven given to men by which we must be saved. *Acts 4:12*

Erin prayed away the screaming demon that had tormented me for years and years, and any other filth that was there. Merv prayed away the spirit of lethargy, then with both hands on my feet, cut those and other evil things off at the root in the name of Jesus.

Merv began praying more specifically for the devil's hold on me to be cut off. I started freaking, thinking we must surely be in for The Exorcist II. The wind rattled the fireplace. I looked up suspiciously, and caught Mum's quick glance at the fireplace. So I hadn't imagined it. Yes, I thought; be afraid. Be very afraid, but nothing happened. It was all peace and calm.

For all I had been through, I'd never seen anything like this. They were dealing with spiritual powers of darkness but there was no foulness or fear, just peace, authority and love. Humbled and grateful, I felt a huge load had lifted. I felt energised, and had a real appreciation of the beauty of the human spirit and of the kindness of these people. I hadn't seen such selflessness. They were meeting to pray for others, and to sing to God. There was nothing of themselves in it. I didn't know it, but I was beginning to see the Holy Spirit at work through his people.

It was very different, and very beautiful.

None of it really meant that much to me at the time because I didn't understand it. But I trusted, and if the things they had cut off and got rid of were really gone, that would be a miracle. I didn't feel a dramatic awakening at the time, or have an impressive experience when I accepted Jesus into my heart. But I went home feeling perhaps a little more peaceful.

Little did I know, the following two weeks were to be my personal Battle of Bastogne. The reality was, I had just made the most significant decision of my life. Wow, did you hear that? Reality! I had made the epic journey from the kingdom of darkness to the kingdom of light. If I died now, I would go to heaven. A bona fide spiritual transaction had taken place within my spirit, the eternal part of me, when I had genuinely repented of my sins and accepted Jesus Christ.

But the enemy of my soul was not pleased. I had served him well.

And I will build my church, and the gates of hell will not overcome it. *Matthew 16:18*

಄಄ ಄಄

11.  The wild side

2001

I went to sleep and dreamed again. I looked up to check on Roq, not prepared for what I saw. His bed was smothered with a big blanket covering it completely. Panic responded to this ugly statement. Mum entered the room. I asked her where Roq was, and she calmly pulled out Roq's stroller from under my bed. Roq had been folded up in his stroller and shoved under my bed. He wasn't breathing. His life returned after heart massage. It was so real. I awoke in a cold sweat, terrified that he was dead or broken and dying somewhere. Would I find him in time? Slowly I realised it had been a nightmare. Or something.

You have enemies? Good.
That means you've stood up for something, sometime in your life.
Winston Churchill

What was it with my dreams these days? I'd always had nightmares and night terrors, but this was taking it to the next level. They were not like dreams at all, but real experiences in a parallel dimension. Night after night I was barraged with evil visions of the many and varied ways in which Roq was going to die, of menacing warnings that if I didn't change my goody–

good ways I was asking for trouble. In my 'dreams', household items came to life and flew around the room. Nothing I could do seemed to block the relentless battery from the realm of the unforgiven. Mum and Dad were woken night after night by my bloodcurdling screams. I became too afraid to turn out the light and go to sleep.

Sometimes I couldn't scream. I was paralysed from the brain down. I hated those the most, the dreams when you try to run, but you can't; try to call out, but you can't get the words out.

I reluctantly gave up the battle to stay awake, and fell asleep. Around 1 a.m I heard a truck slowing down, getting ready to stop at our gate. I knew something was coming, and told myself I'd better get up while I could still move. I didn't want to be caught like a sitting duck as usual, but was just too tired, and the gap of time I thought I had instantly vanished. The truck pulled to a stop at the gate; the door opened and the hellish hitchhiker disembarked. It shuffled down the drive, past my room. I listened to it come in through the back door and shuffle through the laundry. I tried to get up, but I couldn't move and couldn't cry out.

Then I saw it. It walked past my doorway and down towards Mum and Dad's room. Whew! Maybe it wasn't coming for me this time. Then it turned and came back, hunting me. It was undead — an apparition shaped like a tall man, covered in a sheet like a middle-eastern burqa. It lurched toward me. Its face was a black hole. The sheet was empty. Evil gave it form.

I tried again to scream and move, but found myself totally frozen with fear. In slow motion, I watched as it limped toward me. Its arms stretched out slowly to grab me by the throat. In utter rage and frustration I broke through, reached up and grabbed it by the neck, trying to strangle it with my bare hands, but it was like trying to lay hold of a waft of smoke. It fell onto me and dissolved. Had it disappeared when it hit the Holy Spirit in me, or had Mary been called to pray? God knows.

Even though I walk through the darkest valley, I will fear no evil, for you are with me; your rod and your staff, they comfort me. *Psalm 23:4*

ೋ⊙ೋ ⊙ೋ

The next morning after breakfast I looked at Dad. Faithful, loving and often the first one to come running. I wondered how he was handling the supernatural extravaganza.

"Aren't you scared about demons coming into the house every night?" I asked.

"No. They're not coming for me, are they?"

We laughed hard, but it was no joke. Roq also was severely harassed by demonic forces. The rendezvous of innocence and filth in another dimension were marked by his frequent episodes of lashing out and seemingly fighting for his life as he slept tore at my heart. Roq was suffering for my foolish mistakes that had opened spiritual doors that only Jesus could close, and it took time.

The next night Roq was woken once again by the dark side and couldn't be consoled. I took him into my bed and fell asleep with him in the crook of my arm. An hour later I was rudely awoken by the crystal clear knowledge that my arm had moved, and I hadn't moved it. Something ungodly had. I snapped awake instantly as I felt my arm being picked up and moved off him, as if to extricate Roq from me and whisk him away. I couldn't open my eyes or get the word out that is pure power, Jesus, as I battled the heavy demonic oppression. What felt like tons of pressure on my chest prohibited all utterance as completely as though I had been buried alive. I tried to scream to the moon and back, but there was nothing except an impenetrable blanket of fear. It took time, but eventually I got the word out, "JESUS!" I was instantly and irrevocably released; the power of evil severed like a hot knife through butter by the ultimate weapon in the cosmos.

I greatly feared for Roq's life. Somewhere deep down I knew the evil one wasn't allowed to physically hurt us, but when was it going to stop? I was totally worn down and the visions and spiritual attacks were terrifyingly real. In unbearable agony of soul, my heart reached out to the King of Kings and the Lord of Lords. In the spirit, I saw Jesus come and stand in front of me as I held Roq in my arms. Beautiful, peaceful Jesus held his arms out to me — the holes in his hands speaking of love indescribable.

I passed Roq over, into the holy hands of the living God. Jesus' loving smile and unequalled authority reassured and comforted us as he held Roq close to his heart. He was in Jesus' hands now. I knew Roq was going to be ok.

Neither death nor life, neither angels or demons, neither the present nor the future, nor any powers, neither height nor depth, nor anything else in all creation, will be able to separate you from the love of God that is in Christ Jesus our Lord. *Romans 8:38*

We had been through two weeks of relentless demonic attack and were all exhausted. Mum and Mary realised we needed to ask God to fight for us. Satan had become our focus and our eyes had been drawn away from the only one worth looking at. I'd been trying to fight a spiritual battle in my own strength. Mum taught me to pray and to ask Jesus to protect us using scripture as a weapon of warfare — a spiritual sword. She sat up till after 1 a.m, praying through the hours when we usually had the most violation.

Finally, peace.

For the word of God is alive and active. Sharper than any double-edged sword. *Hebrews 4:12*

From hard, cold experience, I found that, in the midst of a spiritual attack, my mind went blank and my body trembled on the inside like a jellyfish. I had to have a strategy. I printed several scriptures out in large print and stuck them to the walls around the room. I read the scriptures out loud when things got ugly and they dealt the punishment instantly and without fail.

> I have given you authority to trample on snakes
> and scorpions and to overcome all the power of the
> enemy; nothing will harm you. *Luke 10:19*
>
> No weapon forged against you will prevail, and
> you will refute every tongue that accuses you. This
> is the heritage of the servants of the Lord, and this
> is their vindication from me," declares the Lord.
> *Isaiah 54:17*

If I couldn't read a scripture, I'd just force the name of Jesus out and that would be enough. When I used the name 'God' or 'Lord' when under attack, I found it didn't work as a weapon.

> Then Jesus came to them and said, "All authority in
> heaven and on earth has been given to me.
> *Matthew 28:18*
>
> The battle is the Lords. *1 Samuel 17:47*

I learned that God the Father is God, God and Jesus are one and the Holy Spirit is one with them. It's part of the mystery that we can't fully understand with our natural minds. The Father is the heart of God (he is in heaven on the throne of grace). Jesus is the face of God (he is seated at the right hand of the Father). The Holy Spirit is the hands and feet of God (he is here with us on earth — our helper). They are one, but have different functions.

The Father gave all authority to his Son, Jesus Christ, when he died for our sins on the cross and rose again from the dead. It is Jesus' name that carries the power. Not Muhammad, not Buddha, not Mother Earth, not The Universe, not Mary the mother of Jesus, not any of the innumerable deities, gods, gurus, ancestors, and good teachers people believe in.

Therefore God exalted him to the highest place
and gave him the name that is above every name,
that at the name of Jesus every knee should bow,
in heaven and on earth and under the earth and
every tongue acknowledge that Jesus Christ
is Lord, to the glory of God the Father.
Philippians 2:9–10

I discovered another weapon, worship. I listened to worship music and thanked God in my heart instead of focusing on Satan. I learned about the power in the blood of Jesus. Just as Jesus' name carries great power, so does the blood he spilled for us when he was crucified in our stead. This sounds weird, but when we 'cover ourselves in the blood of Jesus' in prayer, it actually is so in the spiritual realm. So when evil looks at us, all it can see is the blood of Jesus the Christ, and he is the only one they can't mess with. It's all about Jesus.

The harassment slowed right down after learning these things and praying for God to protect us, but they still happened every now and then. It took a long time to close all the doors and find my identity and authority in Christ. God was teaching me to fight. Not everyone experiences the dark side to this degree when they decide to follow Jesus, but Roq and I did. Perhaps it was because I'd made so many bad choices and opened so many black doors. Perhaps He needed us to have experience in these matters so as to help others in times ahead.

God is real. He had well and truly answered the big question I'd asked in my heart on the couch that day. I couldn't deny the evil I had experienced, and how powerless I was in the face of it. But now I knew the only one who wasn't. The one who has defeated the armies of hell. I couldn't deny the power of Jesus' name and his blood.

To the only God our Saviour be glory, majesty,
power and authority, through Jesus Christ our Lord,
before all ages, now and forevermore! *Jude 1:25*

Everybody has an eternity. It's where we spend it that's the issue. No matter where we end up, eternity is a long time. We seem to think of eternity as some point far ahead in the distant mists of our lives and often don't understand it is a thin line that runs parallel with every step we take. A thin line — which can be crossed easily any given moment.

Before I asked Jesus to be my Lord, I didn't care about that. I just didn't care. My eyes were blind to the truth and reality of the afterlife. I joked about Hell and Armageddon, or 'Arma-gonna-ged-it', with no real understanding of what it meant. It was easy to marginalise Hell as the world we're living in today or some equally erroneous construct and not some actual place where once we arrive there's no leaving, only a living and conscious torture of the body, soul and spirit in a place with no doors and no end.

My journey had begun; a journey like no other. A journey in which I would learn what it meant to walk with God.

He has shown you, O mortal, what is good. And what does the LORD require of you? To act justly and to love mercy and to walk humbly with your God. *Micah 6:8*

༄ঔ୧ ৩ঔ৸

The world appeared more beautiful than before — colours more vibrant, birdsong clear and melodic. Mum taught me all over again to see the simple things and the beauty in nature. The pieces of my heart began to lift and swirl in the updraft of the Holy Spirit. God was beginning to take the ashes of my life and give his beauty in return. The Holy Spirit had been given permission to make his home in me and was slowly changing the way I saw and heard, thought and acted.

I'd been in Ruawai about a month by now. I still had a lot of crying to do over Mark. My heart was thoroughly smashed. I cried in bed. I cried when I drove the car. I cried at the checkout. I cried at the dinner table. I cried until I thought I would be sick and break in two.

The phone rang. It was Mark.

"When are you coming back?"

"Well, I need to talk to you about that. Can you come up?" I said.

"I'll come tomorrow." Click.

Ok, it was obvious what I was going to say, but I didn't want to say it over the phone.

I asked my pastor to come and pray with me before Mark arrived. Erin Underwood was sick in bed. Nevertheless he got up and drove to our place, his eyes bugging at the speedometer swinging wildly backward and forward although he was only driving slowly. Pulling to a stop in the driveway, he let out a sigh of relief and closed the door on the old car.

Over coffee, we talked. Suddenly I realised Mark had arrived and Erin busted out a prayer.

Mark wouldn't come in so I introduced the two men as Erin went to leave. He tried to start his car; it refused to start. Mark spotted Roq's car seat in the garage and began installing it in the Terrano.

While Erin wrestled with his car, Mark impatiently roared off up the road. Eventually, Erin's car coughed to life and he waved and left. Mark returned when he was ready and plonked himself back down on the stairs, his back my stony greeting. I scooped Roq up. Roq reeled back and clutched my neck with both arms.

"Hi," I said, "are you going to come in?" my heart going out to him.

"Are you coming?"

"No. Come in so I can tell you what's been happening."

"I've got things to do." He stalked to the Terrano, ripped the car seat out of the back and threw it onto the driveway. My heart breaking again, I turned away and went inside.

From the bedroom window, I watched Mark reverse up the driveway at speed and the picture of Jesus fall to the floor before my eyes. Mark was gone.

In my heart I ran, but grief overtook me. I fell into Mum's chair in the kitchen, shutting off my emotions as best I could for fear they would kill me. Sharp stabbing, burning pains speared my chest that terrible afternoon. The following day they were still falling like showers of hot fireworks, burning and slowing dying.

This must be what it was to die of a broken heart.

He has prepared his deadly weapons; he makes ready his flaming arrows. *Psalm 7:13*

In addition to all this, take up the shield of faith, with which you can extinguish all the flaming arrows of the evil one. *Ephesians 6:16*

A while later, the phone rang. It was Mark.

"We are really over, aren't we?"

"We're on different trains now, going opposite directions. You can get on mine, but I can't get on yours. The only hope for us is if you give your heart to Jesus."

I may as well have asked Mark to walk on the moon. I slept fitfully with the light on, alternating between crying and dozing.

The weeks passed and the time for Mark to go to jail was near. I knew he would just go and leave the flat and everything as it was. Things were unfinished. I had to go back and help Mark pack and get his stuff into storage, clean up and get out of our lease in the proper way. I packed up Roq and off we went.

Mark and I worked together packing and getting things sorted while Roq played. Mark was happy, no doubt also thinking there was a chance I wouldn't be able to leave again. I knew, however; there was no going back to him.

> Sir, my concern, is not whether God is on our side;
> my greatest concern is to be on God's side, for God is always right.
> *Abraham Lincoln*

Sunday came and I was thoroughly desperate to get to church.

"Will you come to church with me?" I asked Mark.

"You go. I'll stay here."

Roq and I headed towards the church I'd been to with Mum. Or tried. I struggled with some kind of amnesia and drove around in confusion for ages, wasting our precious gas in vain. I became more and more panicky and upset. I finally gave up, and stopped at a random church I passed on the way. I grabbed Roq and my Bible and rushed to the front door. A large guy who looked like a bouncer intercepted me as I tried to enter.

"Can I help you?" he asked.

"I've come for Mass," I told him, moving to go forward as I was already late and didn't want to miss any more. He stepped forward, blocking my path. I could see people sitting inside and was desperate to join them. I didn't know Mass was a Catholic word. I wasn't really even a Catholic, I just wanted to go to a church service.

"Sorry, we can't help you," he said. I went to step around him and go in, but again he blocked my path. Beyond upset and confused, I wept all the way back to the flat. When Mark asked what was wrong, I cried harder, trying to explain. He tried to humour me but could see he thought it was a big fuss over nothing. I frantically surfed the TV channels until I found a church service and soaked it up with great relief.

I was swimming against the tide again. That night I went to sleep and had another nasty vision. I was in the kitchen with my back to the stove when without warning the stove morphed into a black hole and almost snatched me away like a silent tornado. Mark stood in front of me holding Roq in his arms, just watching. I reached out to Roq and woke up sweating.

I had been warned. Do the job, and get out.

Dad arrived to help move stuff to the storage units with Mark, and I cleaned the flat. We piled our clothes, Roq's things, and the kitchen stuff into Dad's van to take with us. The move finished and bond was received.

We said our goodbyes.

He lifted me out of the slimy pit, out of the mud and mire; he set my feet on a rock and gave me a firm place to stand. *Psalm 40:2*

---

12. Miracles

2001

Mary was excited to tell us some guest speakers were coming to town. Trevor and Jan Yaxley were going to speak at the town hall on a winters Sunday in 2001.

'Who? Never heard of them. I don't know what this straight, old couple would talk about but it sure wouldn't be anything that would interest me,' the narrator ranted. I was still a little rough around the edges. It's just as well that when God gently sets us at the starting line of the journey with him, he is patient. No one ever 'arrives' this side of heaven; it's a process and some have further to travel than others. It takes time to stop conforming to the patterns of this world and to be transformed by the renewing of our minds *(Romans 12:2)*. It takes time for the old to pass away and the new to come.

Fear, shame, negativity and grief still attempted daily hostile takeovers of my mind, and reconciling who I had been with who I was now was no small feat as the gap was like the Grand Canyon. I'd always struggled to find my identity, so it was better than Christmas finding out who I was as a child of God, His beloved, and the power and promises that were now available to me. I was a new creation in Christ, chosen and redeemed. Loved by God. Saved by grace through faith in Jesus Christ. Restoration is a beautiful thing. And that was just the beginning.

God forgives us our sins, but we also have to forgive ourselves, and often we still have to deal with the consequences. Like accepting you've wasted years of your life, or broken a family, or having to recover from a toxic relationship or habit, or raise a child who wants to know why his Dad is not here — or worse. Some things aren't supernaturally 'healed', but have to be walked through, or fought for and won — one battle at a time. I was finding out that, with God, nothing is wasted, no matter how bad it is, and that battles are fought in God's strength, not ours. And that's a relief.

Reluctantly I went along to the talk with Mum and Mary. The large hall was half filled with people, a magnificent turnout for Ruawai. The entire town must have been there! Not wanting to draw attention to myself, my attitude and I stood together awkwardly at the back by ourselves, leaning against the wall and stared at the floor, listening.

Erin made the introduction and Trevor began. As I listened the sunflower in my heart lifted its face from the floor and looked at the light coming from this authentic, honourable man of God. I'd never heard someone speak so honestly about his life before. It was captivating. Trevor and Jan founded Lifeway College in Snells Beach, and the first course began in 1988. There were incredible stories of living by faith, signs and wonders, miracles, extravagant love, and giving as a lifestyle.

He talked about God from experience. He had my attention. All of a sudden Trevor stopped midstream and pointed to Mary. Our Mary.

"You, what's your name?" he asked.

Mary had been hiding too, so she thought. She couldn't believe Trevor was addressing her and kept looking behind her.

"The one with the glasses on her Bible," Trevor said. "What's your name?"

Appalled at the attention, Mary whispered, "Mary."

"I can see the true Spirit of God working in your life and the lives of others through you."

That was the best thing Mary could have ever heard. It was her purpose, and it was true.

"Does anyone feel the presence of God here?" Trevor asked. To my surprise, my raised hand was one of only two in the air. Trevor acknowledged us.

"The band is going to play now, and the two of you are welcome to join me up the front," he said.

I was shocked and pretended I didn't hear what he said. Ann Dodd made her way to me and suggested perhaps he had meant me, hadn't he? I nodded sheepishly; she put her arm around me, and we went up the front together. Trevor grabbed my hand in both of his.

"You're a good woman," he said to me. He looked at Ann. "She's a good woman, isn't she?" I was surprised Ann nodded, as she definitely knew too much. Ann and Merv had been friends of the family from the beginning. Trevor looked into my eyes and said, "Oh, you've been through hell, haven't you?"

"Yes, and I've still got more to go through yet."

"What's your name? I'll pray for you now."

"As you cried into your pillow, I was there. As you lay on the couch in total despair, I was with you."

God was talking to me. He said something about my bereavement but I wasn't able to concentrate on listening. The more he prayed, the more I cried. As I silently sobbed, a raging torrent ran down my front. Mary was crying too. Mum stood close, smiling and holding Roq.

I was humbled. "Thank you for talking to me," I said.

"Oh no, dear. That's what I live for! Come and see me when you're ready."

◦๏๏ ๏๏◦

We cannot solve problems by using
the same kind of thinking we used when we created them.
Albert Einstein

The tide I'd been swimming against was now blatantly obvious. Everything Mark and I had touched toward the end had turned to crap. As Dad and I delved into the debris from my past, a giant steaming dung heap of bad debt was uncovered. Unpaid speeding and parking fines, power and phone bills; and bills I didn't even know about until I rang the debt collection agency and asked for the ugly truth regarding both Mark and me. There was roughly $6,000 owing to clear our names.

I had the Terrano. Mark didn't need it in jail, and Roq and I needed wheels. It was expensive to run and I needed to replace it with a fuel-efficient vehicle. Unfortunately the warrant of fitness and registration had expired and it needed $1,300 worth of work.

On top of that was THE BIG ONE. The Paradox tax bills that amounted to roughly $26,000. I recoiled from the box of Inland Revenue bills after setting it down on the kitchen table. Dad's eyes bugged out. The years of frustration and striving to find someone at the Inland Revenue Department to help me work through it bubbled to the surface. Along with the weight of all the other problems, it was overwhelming. Familiar freeloaders, hopelessness and despair, tugged at my sleeves reminding me I was screwed.

Then I felt a small nudge in my spirit. "Hey, you've got me now remember?"

With man this is impossible, but with God all things are possible. *Matthew 19:26*

I ran to God and happily piled it all into his lap. He told me it was time to ring Inland Revenue again. I agreed to give it one last shot, made the call and explained the story for the last time.

"Please hold the line, I'll just transfer you to someone who can help," she said after I'd just explained it all for the last time.

"No, please don't! I can't keep explaining it over and over and getting transferred and transferred and no one can ever help me. I'm trying to get this sorted out, and you guys are not helping or trying!" I broke down and cried. Yes! I still had a few tears left for that.

"No, wait," she said kindly. "I'm transferring you to the person who looks after the difficult cases. It's what he does. He'll make an appointment and come to see you."

"Oh, right," I sniffed, "he'll come to see me in Ruawai?" If an Inland Revenue agent visited me in Ruawai, a tiny town most New Zealanders haven't even heard of, that would be all the evidence I needed to believe there really was a God.

"Yes! Yes he will. I'll just put you through now."

The agent made an appointment to see me in Ruawai and outlined the paperwork he needed ready for him. I spent $450 getting copies of bank statements. These days you can download them for free from your online bank vault, but things were different then. Finally I was ready, nervous but ready. And he was at the door.

"Hi, I'm Chris," he said with a friendly smile.

We sat and talked for an hour about God over coffee before we even mentioned my tax. God had sent a Christian Inland Revenue agent.

"Ok, let's have a look," he said finally. "Just give me a little while and I'll have a look at everything," as he surveyed the paperwork.

I left him to it. After a while he sat back and looked at me. I held my breath.

"Well, it looks to me as if what you said is right — the accountant has made a mistake and this GST is not actually owed," he said. Silence. I had a new self-preservation technique. If I had no expectations, I couldn't be disappointed. I was not getting my hopes up. I would celebrate once I'd seen it in writing, then and only then.

Chris understood. "Just give me a couple of days and I'll check it out fully with my supervisor. But I'm pretty sure it's going to be ok."

"Thank you so much."

After a week a new account arrived in the mail. It showed the large opening balance at the top, then the reversal and a balance owing of $0.00.

It was like the pregnancy test all over again; I stared at it for ages but it just wouldn't register. I couldn't believe it was ok now. The giant tax problem was gone! I started to cry. I cried and cried. A few days later I noticed a heavy weight had lifted off my shoulders. I felt different, tangibly lighter.

I took time out and thanked God for His awesome miracle. But he wasn't about to stop there.

One generation commends your works to another; they tell of your mighty acts. *Psalm 145:4*

The Spirit of God was at work cleaning up our financial cesspool one lump at a time. My bank rang me to ask if they could change my accounts as they'd noticed I was paying more in bank fees than I needed to; I then saved $15 per month. This was before the banking market had become so competitive, and this was unheard of. The small things are just as important to God as the big things, and small miracles are no more miraculous than the large ones.

Mum and Dad kept me and Roq for two years as I paid off all the bad debt I could find for Mark and me, then started saving.

Mark and I had owned a couple of Suzuki Magic 50cc motorbikes that I had attempted to sell at the Waitakere flat. Mark was at work and wasn't involved in the sale process. I clearly told the buyer the price per bike. The buyer said he'd take both, paid for one, would pay for the other at a later date, and took both motorbikes. Later, he said he'd been told the price was for both bikes and stubbornly refused to pay for the other bike, or return it. Little did he know, I lived with a beast.

Mark was furious. He took a couple of mates to get the bike back one night. I was awoken the next morning by Mark's question.

"Do you think this needs stitches?" he asked, peeling a sticking plaster off a tummy-turning three-inch gash in his forearm that moved like a toothless grin. While climbing through the freshly smashed window he leant on the broken pane with his forearm thinking it just might hold his weight, until he felt the flesh give way under the weight of his body and the glass hit the bone.

"Yes!" I said loudly, "and antibiotics!" I'm not sure why he asked, as he had no intention of going to the doctor.

"We got there and the neighbour's big Dobermans came running out, barking and snarling, Shane snarled back and they ran off, whimpering. I smashed the garage window and cut my arm getting in. I got the scooter out then the cops turned up and confiscated it. They're keeping it until they can find out what happened."

For months I tried to resolve the issue, but it was another dilemma that supernaturally defied resolution. We were met with open hostility from the cops on the phone, so Mark and I went to the station to try to have a reasonable discussion. Sigh. We were greeted with verbal abuse from a pack of feral police officers, and left with a parking ticket although we had parked legally. Sigh. Again, I had handed it over to God, and again he said it was time to ring.

I rang the Henderson Police Station and was put through to a kind policeman who listened carefully and said he'd look into it for me. Again, I wasn't going to get my hopes up. Then he rang back.

"You can come and pick up your motorbike whenever you like. And I've cancelled the ticket you got when you were here last time." Another miracle.

Dad, Roq and I travelled to Auckland and met up with the kind policeman. Eventually Roq got sick of being in his car seat, and started screaming his lungs out. The policeman looked at Roq.

"Wait, I'll be back in a minute."

A few minutes later he returned with a darling white soft toy puppy with a big black spot on its back. Spot Dog was Roq's favourite for years. As I watched this gentle giant who had taken care of us lean down and show such love to this little mite, I saw the image and character of God.

I sold the motorbike and paid for the repairs to the Terrano. When the Terrano sold, I bought an efficient, reliable yellow van that kept us going for years. God continued effortlessly to put more wrongs to right.

While moving my clothes out of the Waitakere flat, my grandmother's diamond engagement ring had gone missing, to my great distress. Mum and I both found it impossible to come to terms with the loss of this precious heirloom. It had now been lost for two years and it certainly never occurred to either of us that we would ever see it again.

Sitting in the Ruawai Community Church one evening Merv Dodd had a word from God for me:

**"Janet, I have brought you out of the rubbish dump.
I have restored your spiritual inheritance, now I will
restore your natural inheritance."**

Eventually, the time came to sort through my old clothes Dad had stored in his garage for me. Looking at them through new eyes was thoroughly shocking. I might as well have just raided the closet of an anorexic stripper. There was little there of any use at all, so most of it was dispatched straight to the second-hand shop as soon as humanly possible, and preferably under the cover of night.

In the driveway, I unpacked each plastic sack of sheets and blankets one by one, sorting as I went. Finally, I had worked my way to the bottom of the last battered and torn old rubbish bag and picked up the last sheet. There, gleaming like a star in the night sky on the torn black plastic lay my grandmother's engagement ring. And once again, I looked and looked, not believing my eyes.

God sorted the pieces of the puzzle, simultaneously healing my body, soul and spirit. Before long a beautiful mosaic started to take shape amongst the fragments.

And still, the best was yet to come.

When the day of Pentecost came, they were all together in one place. Suddenly a sound like the blowing of a violent wind came from heaven and filled the whole house where they were sitting. They saw what seemed to be tongues of fire that separated and came to rest on each of them. All of them were filled with the Holy Spirit and began to speak in other tongues as the Spirit enabled them. *Acts 2:1-4*

John the Baptist, Jesus' cousin who challenged people to prepare the way for the coming Christ put it this way; "I baptise you with water for repentance. But after me comes one who is more powerful than I, whose sandals I am not worthy to carry. He will baptise you with the Holy Spirit and fire," *(Matthew 3:11)*.

I started reading and hearing about 'being baptised with the Holy Spirit.' I didn't know what it meant, but the Holy Spirit was making sure I was going to find out. I went after it with all my heart, asking God for his baptism of fire.

I had to drive Mark and myself home from a wedding party once in Mark's Corvette; a mean 1974 T-Top with a 464 Chevy beast under the bonnet. That's right, it's not a typo, Mark had a 454 bored out to the max. That was a lot of motor, and no power steering. I'll say it again — no power steering. The weight of the motor fell right on the front axle, making it near impossible for my weakling arms to turn the wheel when the car was stationary. It was easier to turn the wheel when the car was moving, but it was still incredibly difficult.

It's the same with us before we have the Holy Spirit; driving our lives without power steering. It's tough. We manage for a while, but we eventually get tired, grumpy, and we make mistakes. We are not connected to our power source; the source of true wisdom and revelation.

When the day of my Pentecost came, Mum and I were at a women's conference in Matamata. The guest speaker prayed for me with her hands on my head. She was 'praying in tongues' (the heavenly language, praying in the spirit) and suddenly my head began to rapidly heat up. I started to cry as I was filled with an overwhelming revelation of God's love for me, and with power. The temperature of my brain rose rapidly and almost exponentially, from warm to very warm, to supernaturally hot.

I just knew in my heart the Holy Spirit had healed the brain damage from years of drug abuse, and I wept at the love God extended to someone so completely undeserving and for something totally self-inflicted. But that's what grace is.

God is God, and we are not.

But you will receive power when the Holy Spirit comes on you. *Acts 1:8*

---

13. Restoration

2003

It was eighteen months before I was ready to see Trevor. God had resurrected me from the dead and restored my shambolic affairs. I had a new peace, a joy, and Roq and I had hope for a better future. With sins forgiven, eternal life and new strength, I now felt a stirring, a restlessness, and a frustration. I had an insatiable hunger for the things of God that needed intense feeding, but I didn't know what was next. Where to go? What to do? All I knew was where I didn't want to be. Auckland.

Mary popped in with a brochure to show us about Lifeway College. Lifeway had its roots in the Salvation Army, the work of General William Booth and his wife, Catherine. I knew what I had to do. It was time to see Trevor.

I walked into Trevor's office in Snells Beach. "I've got no idea why I'm here," I told him.

"That's fine. I'll get Anna to show you around, and we can go from there," said Trevor, understanding what it was to be led by the Holy Spirit. At 19, Anna was already a leader in the Lifeway Army and had a wisdom beyond her years.

I felt God wanted me to sign up for the Lifeway Army — six months of onsite biblical studies with 'army-flavoured' basic training, culminating in a Certificate in Evangelism. I could study part-time and do the training over a year if I wanted, as I had Roq. I went over the options with Mum and Dad. Then Dad dropped the bombshell.

"I could look after Roq if you want to do the course full-time, and get it done."

Mum still worked full-time; Dad had retired. It made sense to go hard, reduce costs and get it done. I was desperate to learn more about God and find out what I was made of, but the thought of leaving Roq for six months was best not thought about at length. Roq was only three years old, but it had to be done.

I began to prepare for a truly life-changing adventure.

❧❦❧

In the meantime, Dad and I were having an epic power struggle in the kitchen; the small things had begun to irritate us. Things were becoming a little scratchy.

"Why don't you and Roq go and stay at the beach house for a while?" he suggested one day.

"Hmm," I liked the sound of that, so we did. Roq was in heaven in Omamari, a wild and beautiful place on the west coast of New Zealand. It was a special time of healing and play for us both.

Although I lived on the opposite coast, I started having regular prayer ministry with the pastor at Lifeway at the time, Ron Schepers. It was counselling, but with 'power assist.' I crammed five days caregiving work into four, so I could make my weekly migration and spend a couple of hours with Ron. He gave me a book called 'Released from Bondage' by Dr. Neil Anderson, to read a chapter each week for homework. This was a powerful, and shocking collection of stories about people who were freed by the power of Jesus from demonic and emotional bondage, abuse or occult influences. At the back was a comprehensive list to check through and renounce of what entangles us in the dark side, from everyday features such as horoscopes, psychic readings, occult games and Wicca, through to satanic ritual abuse. The Steps to Freedom at the back of the book kicked butt and slammed some dark spiritual doors shut.

This intense repentance and restoration took time. There was so much for which to ask forgiveness. At times I was overwhelmed by the amount of sin to plough through, and wondered how I could even remember it all to repent of it. But that's God's business: and as he brought things up in my memory, I confessed them one by one to God and received healing and forgiveness. I wrote a letter to Mark's daughter Danielle, and her mother, to say that I was sorry and to ask their forgiveness. I rang Josh and did the same.

The enemy of my soul didn't take all this lying down. All hell broke loose once again, except this time, Roq and I were on our own.

I will train your hands for battle. *Psalm 18:34*

I had scripture hung around the bedroom walls in large print, and I sure needed it. Once again, Roq and I suffered major demonic harassment, usually at night, and time and again I was called to fight. Continuous opportunities were given to make me strong in the face of opposition. It was terrifying for us both, but God prevailed every time. While dozing one day my arm was once again picked up and thrown into a different position by a demonic entity; another time, my foot was moved.

Be alert and of sober mind. Your enemy the devil prowls around like a roaring lion looking for someone to devour. *1 Peter 5:8*

I stood firm, and refused to be put off track. The roaring lion is toothless when it comes face to face with the name of Jesus Christ. Fear and deception are his only weapons. I cast my cares and concerns upon God, kept my eyes on Him, and kept moving forward with my mission to be freed from the spiritual problems that bound.

Children and animals are very sensitive to the spiritual world, and can often see things that adults can't see with our hardened consciences. I was brushing my teeth one day when Roq came screaming into the bathroom in utter terror, and clung to my leg for dear life.

"There's a man in my room!" he screamed.

It was broad daylight, but I knew it was demonic. Sure enough, when I went in I couldn't see anyone. I commanded it to go in the name of Jesus the Christ.

"How did he get in?" Roq asked, badly shaken.

I knew I couldn't tell him. Knowing would be worse than not knowing at all. Ron had advised me of my mandate, and now was the time to use it.

> I have given you authority to trample on snakes and scorpions and to overcome all the power of the enemy; nothing will harm you. *Luke 10:19*

"I think it's important you think about getting water baptised," Ron said one day. "It really makes a statement in the spiritual realm."

I certainly needed all the help I could get. Water baptism is symbolic of the death, burial and resurrection of Christ. The immersion of the body symbolises the old self with its sinful desires dying in the baptismal water, being buried in Christ and receiving new life when raised from the water as Christ did upon his resurrection.

> We were, therefore, buried with him through baptism into death in order that, just as Christ was raised from the dead through the glory of the Father, we too may live a new life. For if we have been united with him in a death like his, we will certainly also be united with him in a resurrection like his. For we know that our old self was crucified with him so that the body ruled by sin might be done away with, that we should no longer be slaves to sin. *Romans 6:4-6*

One cold, autumn day in April 2003 after sharing my story at Lifeway Church, a small group stood together on the shore at Martins Bay under a low ceiling of soft, grey cloud. As Ron lifted me from my baptismal dunking, it seemed as though God himself poked a finger through the cloud and bathed us all in a beautiful, strong ray of warming sunshine.

"God has put a seal on you that no one can take away. You are God's daughter. God has engraved your name on the palm of His hand," Ron said. "I saw the seal. It's quite large and very thick, and everything in the spirit realm can see it."

"God is pleased today," said Mary.

"If anyone is in Christ, they are a new creation. The sun (Son) is on your life, and you have an awesome destiny; the potential for good is way beyond you now. He will take you from platform to platform, if you stay close to him. You will be able to take the word of God into the hardened areas," another prophesied.

Ann and Merv Dodd conveyed the precious message with which they had been entrusted:

"My child, I have lifted you from the mire and placed your feet upon the rock where you are now a sweet-smelling fragrance for me. As you stay close to me and learn from me, I will lead you into impossible places for me and my glory, but you must stay close to me, trust me, and obey me; even in the face of opposition.
My child, my love for you is overflowing, and this love will touch the lives of many people for they see the change in you and rejoice."

⁓⁕⁓

Back in Ruawai, I sat at the kitchen table studying the application form for the Army training at Lifeway College. My stomach dropped as I read the next question: DO YOU HAVE A CRIMINAL RECORD?

'Well, that's that! I'm screwed! I'm a criminal,' said my narrator. I grabbed my keys and jumped into the van, thinking I'd better check my facts.

Pulling up outside the Ruawai Police Station, I took a deep breath.

"Can I help you?" the pleasant country copper greeted me with a smile.

"Hi. I am applying for college, and need to know if I have a criminal record please." I smiled sweetly.

"Sure thing, won't be a minute," he said helpfully, turning to the computer.

I watched his expression darken in front of my eyes. His friendly, smiling eyes were gone and he stared at me with a hard, flat expression.

"It says *'kidnapping'* here!" he glared accusingly.

"Oh. That was just a misunderstanding."

"That's not what it says here!"

"Oh. Is that all?" I squeaked.

"Isn't that enough?"

"Oh yea, I guess," I said backing out, his eyes tracking me.

I collapsed back into the kitchen chair in front of my application. Under the criminal convictions heading I wrote, 'I only have one criminal conviction: kidnapping.'

A $50 deposit was required with my application, but I enclosed $500 along with a note saying, 'Just in case you accept kidnappers.' I might as well have a laugh since I was going to be rejected anyway. To my surprise I was accepted, and six weeks later I had the clearest feeling of coming home as I drove down Goodall Road and pulled to a stop outside the dining hall at Lifeway College. Anna, who turned out to be one of the leaders for my intake, was sitting on the dining hall steps and we looked at each other through the windscreen and laughed. It was as if she knew what a mission it had been just getting there. My things were loaded in the back of the van, and I was ready for registration.

'Time for a nice cup of tea and a lie down,' I thought. But this was army style training based on New Zealand Army disciplines, and we started as we meant to continue, straight into it. Shortly after registration I found myself in a world of pain, enduring the RFL along with the rest of my intake. I can't say exactly 'alongside' my intake; they were long gone, leaving me lucky last and gasping for air like a beached groper. RFL stands for Required Fitness Level. It doesn't sound too painful, just three little words.

However, my fitness level couldn't be measured. I didn't have one. This was Survivor: Bible College, and I was in big trouble.

The hilly mile and a half run was nasty, and of course I was last to finish. No surprises there. When I finally dragged my butt back up to the line, my narrator commented, 'the show's over people, go back to your normal lives.' At thirty-six years old I was the oldest in my intake, and the official Nana. Ages ranged from sixteen to twenty-six. I have to stop here and acknowledge the urban legend, Shirley. This unforgettably beautiful New Zealand grandmother completed the Lifeway Army training in her seventies.

I'd been fit at school, and into my early twenties, but once I got my first car, it was all over. It's fair to say, the next twenty years of hard-core chemical abuse and no exercise at all may have had an effect also. After the run, we did as many sit-ups and press-ups as we could. For me of course, that didn't take long. My first and only girl-press-up ended in a face-plant. It doesn't get any worse than that. Our numbers, or lack thereof, were recorded, to be used in evidence against us. Boot camp had officially started.

I fell into bed at the end of the first day with my boots on, after heeding the warning to pack my backpack and be ready to go. Where? That was on a need-to-know basis, and we didn't need to know. About 1 a.m, the blower ripped through the still atmosphere like a nuclear event. It was one of those heinous air horns that made you want to rip the offender's arm off and bludgeon him over the head with it until he stopped twitching. The kind that should be limited to ocean liners in the fog. I was ready as soon as I stood up. I'd slept in my clothes.

"Form up outside in five minutes. If anyone is late, there will be privileges." That meant the privilege of doing penalty press-ups, or repeating the whole process until you come in on time, while your team enjoyed privileges. I was on time, and my prohibitive conscience ensured I was on time every time, and gave myself permission to die trying. They were easing us into it gently. We were on our way. Several hours later, we arrived at Puketi Forest in the Far North.

"Ready for a nice coffee now," I thought as I manoeuvred my imitation prosthetic limbs out of the van.

"Form up!" a leader barked. He gave us brief instructions. We were to learn fast, listen very carefully to instructions, and wait until we heard the full instructions before running off. The ability to listen, it seems, doesn't come naturally. We were divided into groups of four. Each group was to carry a heavy picnic table around the cabin in under two minutes, and come in smiling. We failed several times before we came in under time, and then once again before we came in under time, and smiling.

After lunch we tackled an Adventure Based Learning game (ABL); the Hole in the Wall. Ropes threaded between two trees left small gaps. The objective was to post our entire team through a small hole about head height, without any part of any body touching the rope at all, including hair and clothing. The hardest part was getting the first and last ones through, as there was no one on the other side to help. If anyone accidently touched the rope, we all started again after doing a few sets of press-ups and star jumps. The name of the game was Teamwork. Personalities and human nature soon came to the fore, making for an interesting psychology case study.

We finally got the team through, and celebrated. We'd won! We were the champions. We could relax and watch the other team suffer. But, no. There are no champions; there is only 'the Team.' That is all of us, every last one. Groups or individuals don't count. This is how we should be in life, how it used to be when people cared about each other, before self became king. It was quite the paradigm shift.

We got straight on with helping the other team get the rest of their guys through. The other game was called Perseverance. After we'd all succeeded we had to do it again, this time in under twenty minutes. Whenever we took too long, we did more press-ups and started again. No time for a cup of tea and a lie down there either.

Although this took most of the afternoon there was still time for a PT (physical training) session before dinner. We formed up into two lines for a run down the forest road. We eventually came to an intersection and ran it in a U-turn to start the way back again. Except it wasn't a U-turn, it was a circle. We ran around and around the intersection in circles until someone realised there was a piece of rubbish on the road and picked it up. Somehow I just knew we would have run the circle all night if nobody had noticed the rubbish. We ran, stopping often to do press-ups and sit-ups on the road. My hands and knees became so bruised and raw from the gravel road, it wasn't long before I had to do proper guy press-ups to save my knees. The skin on my palms quickly became thick with callouses.

By the end of the night we had to know everyone's full names, failing that of course, came privileges. There were thirty-five of us, not counting the five leaders. My intake included people from Singapore, Japan, Australia, Canada, the United States, Latvia, and all over New Zealand. It was a clever way to counter the clique.

By the end of the first day I wasn't sure what had hit me, but whatever it was, it was big. I was shattered, and missed Roq desperately. The vast expanse of training stretched before me like a nuclear holocaust. Considering all that had happened in just this first full day, I wasn't overly enthusiastic about the idea of another one hundred and eighty days like this one. You could say this was a definite low point for me.

In the cabin after dinner one of our leaders, the college Dean, taught on attitude. Very appropriate! Passive rebellion: the act of internally complaining and harbouring resentment is as bad as open rebellion. This was a major battle for me as I was continually challenged to endure hardship like a good solider *(2 Timothy 2:3).* Deep-seated anger surfaced from years of unhappiness, and I was tempted to take it out on the people around me.

Passive rebellion is something that festers away largely unchallenged in our society, and is very destructive. It totally hinders any work the Holy Spirit is doing, not to mention the physiological and relational damage it causes. Now the training is over :) I'm so grateful for the opportunity to practically learn about passive rebellion. And by practically learn, I mean battle with it under severe circumstances day after day until I mastered it, and it doesn't have a place in my life any more. Well, not for long anyway. The way I roll now when I strike an ugly attitude is to wrestle through it with God, and not move until I'm sorted.

Above all else, guard your heart, for everything you do flows from it. *Proverbs 4:23*

Girls slept in the cabin, guys in the big tent. Sleeping soundly later that night was easy until our collective consciousness was shattered in the small hours by the blower releasing a payload of adrenaline into our veins. It didn't do much for your demeanour. We had one minute to be dressed and formed up outside, fully ready to tramp. Again, if we were late we all went back and did it again until everyone was on time. We stood at attention for five minutes. Anyone who scratched or moved got press-ups. We were dismissed to go back to bed after that, but slept on eggshells waiting for the blower to rip us a new one again, without warning. This was a recurring nightmare every night we spent at the cabin.

The next time it blew was 5.30 a.m. One minute to be formed up out the front. It was straight into a full-on hour of PT under the stars before breakfast. After breakfast we headed off into the bush with our full packs for what was to be a thirty-six hour hike. The first night they were easy on us and we got to sleep right through.

The second night one of the leaders, Peter Meafou, staged a broken leg and we had to manufacture a stretcher out of bush material and raincoats, and carry him out. Pete was a massive Tongan, seemingly carved from solid granite, and an A-grade rugby player. He was a beast. Whenever he played in the annual staff-versus-student rugby game, people were reluctant to tackle him, simply parting like the Red Sea.

We had to administer first aid. I prayed that he would be healed; stuffed if I would carry him out. He wasn't healed. We carried him out.

We had one person on each corner of the stretcher, and subs ready when it got too tough. Someone else (me) went ahead and lit the way by torchlight, while leading the team in cadences (scripture based) non-stop to encourage them. I only had one torch, so quickly perfected walking backwards through the wild bush in the dark, so that I could shine the light on the ground in front of the team. We spent most of the second night carrying Pete out. We had no idea where we were, or how many more hours or days it was going to be before we got back to the cabin.

I consider that our present sufferings are not worth comparing with the glory that will be revealed in us.
Romans 8:18

When I felt at my worst and wallowed alone in my bad attitude I sank even lower; but when I pushed through and encouraged someone, even if all I could manage was a simple smile, I gained heavenly strength.

It was just before the sun started thinking about coming up, and our mouths were just hanging open, when one of our leaders put it to us. We had the option of sleeping where we were, or carrying on. I chose to sleep where I was: standing up. But there was one kamikaze in our midst, Lisa Kroon, who screamed 'NO! We keep going!' So we did.

Five minutes later we stumbled into the cabin.

We stayed in Puketi Forest for several days. We spent our time doing ABLs, PT twice a day, being blown out of our bunks all hours of the night, and downloading from the leaders.

Sore didn't quite cover it. I had rigor mortis. The pain was excruciating just trying to move about gently, not that we had that luxury. Mostly it was a case of having one second to get from A to B with limbs that no longer bent. I could hardly reach my boots to get them on, so I slept in them every night, soaking wet and muddy. This is where I made my critical mistake: buying cheap running shoes and hiking boots. Did I say hiking boots? I meant steel capped men's work boots. Yep. And did I say running shoes? I meant lame as, cheap dress sneakers. That's what wrecked me the most at boot camp. They were two of the worst miscalculations I've ever made, and that's really saying something. The boots were so heavy, when saturated and muddy, I had to manually lift my legs over fallen trees with my hands one at a time because I couldn't lift them by themselves. They had absolutely no grip, and I constantly slipped and pulled my thigh muscles, and then there were the blisters. At the very first opportunity I crawled to the nearest sports shop and spent $600 on a great pair of running shoes, quality hiking boots, and proper thermals. It was the best money I have ever spent.

It was the last night of boot camp in Puketi Forest. We'd had the choice of going to the hot pools and having a soak or staying at the cabin, or cooking dinner for everyone. It sounds like a no-brainer, but I chose to stay and cook with one of the guys, Chris Apanui. I had the feeling that if I got into a hot pool and relaxed, I'd have to be stretchered out. We had so much fun talking that we nearly burnt the cabin down, and our eyes looked like a crime against nature from the smoke.

After dinner and some teaching we hit the bunks for what seemed like five seconds before the blower went off. One minute to be formed-up out the front in full hiking gear. Well that was easy now; we'd had enough practice, and we never took our gear off. Five minutes, I thought, and I'll be back in the sack. Five minutes later we were back in the sack, only to repeat the process again after we'd all just got back to sleep. The third time was also a surprise in more ways than one. We stood motionlessly at attention, waiting for the word in the freezing, driving rain. And waiting. And waiting. And waiting. As I stared at the cabin window the wood in between the panes of glass began to look like the cross Jesus hung on. As I hung out with Jesus, time and cold lost their power.

For just as we share abundantly in the sufferings of Christ, so also our comfort abounds through Christ.
2 Corinthians 1:5

After forty-five minutes, Martin Hulse fell to his knees, then sideways with his hands still behind his back in a dead faint, but still at attention. He came to fairly quickly when his face hit the huge puddle in which he then did his press-ups. Then another one fell, not wanting to be outdone. The blood runs to your legs when you stand a long time without moving, and your head goes dizzy. It helps to clench and unclench the muscles in your thighs, but hindsight is a fine thing. The guys didn't have the luxury of a cabin; their tent had been flooded days back, and their gear saturated through. They had very few reserves left.

After one full hour standing in the winter storm we were released to go to bed, however the blower sounded again around 5 a.m for PT. In the end I was dreaming of PT when I slept, and had moments where I wasn't sure whether I was awake or asleep, or on P and having another psychotic episode. Angela Scott had obviously been sleeping well until she fell out of the third-story bunk and hit the deck hard. If it wasn't the blower waking us all up, it was girls falling from the sky.

During the last tramp in Puketi Forest, the hard-cores were invited to go the extra mile and do some abseiling for fun. I opted to collapse where I stood for a power nap. I was sure time had ceased to move forward and we were caught in a cosmic loop that had no end, but eventually we piled into the vans for the journey back to Snells Beach. Sitting down and snoozing just felt too good to be true. As we neared the Brynderwyn turnoff, we took an unexpected detour close to Mum and Dad's house. I began to struggle severely being so close to Roq, and not being able to see him. Who knew when I was going to be able to see him again? It was heart-breaking.

Out of the blue, I heard God speak audibly in my ear.

"So you think you've sacrificed so much, leaving Roq for a little while, and keep going on about how much you've given up. What if I asked you to leave Roq with your parents for good, so you can do my work?"

I knew I couldn't mess with God, or give a superficial answer. I had to really go there, and decide. It took me a full five minutes to come to terms with the concept, and genuinely agree to it, or not. Oblivious to the company in the van, I gave God my answer. Out loud.

"Ok."

The second it came out of my mouth, I heard God's answer.

"Good. Now you won't have to."

I let go a large sigh of deep relief. God had tested me, and I had passed. I had nothing to complain about anymore, it was time to suck it up. He had asked Abraham to literally sacrifice his long-awaited, first-born son at the dawn of the age, to test his obedience and make sure God was first in his life *(Genesis 22:1-18)*. Abraham followed God's instruction without question, and without hesitation. At the very last moment, an angel stopped Abraham from sacrificing Isaac. God does not require or condone child sacrifice; it is an abomination to him. It was simply a test. My test put things into perspective for me pretty quickly. I would be grateful for whatever time I may or may not get with Roq during the course of this training. That, however, didn't quench the unbelievable ache in our hearts, or the rivers of tears we both cried, but what we both gained from this training was priceless.

I found Roq's Buzzy Bee neck cushion in the van, put it around my neck and went to sleep in the back, as one of the leaders drove us home. We pulled up at a gas station and I did my best Shaun of the Dead impression to the counter, bleary-eyed and caked in mud to forage for chocolate.

"Can I help you?" the startled cashier asked. My friend, Sienna Thompson, started laughing. I was scaring the children.

"You've still got the Buzzy Bee on your neck!" she squeaked through hysteria. Who knew there were Buzzy Bee zombies in these parts now?

After what seemed like an age, we arrived back at Lifeway, ending the official Longest Week of My Life. After we packed down, to my immense relief and utter amazement, we were dismissed for the weekend. I got straight into my van without changing clothes, and drove the seventy-five minutes to see Roq.

I pulled up at Ruawai, but couldn't haul my sorry ass up the stairs, so I just stood in the drive looking at the front door. I didn't even have the option of coming at it, at speed. Mum and Dad opened the door to see me in the same muddy bush clothes I'd been in all week, trying again to get up the stairs without bending my legs. Mum and Dad looked me and blinked. Dad looked at Mum. Mum looked at Dad. They both looked at me and realised they had to help me up the stairs. Mum reckons there's been two occasions in my life when she should have taken a photo. The first one was my impression of Edvard Munch's painting 'The Scream', when I first arrived back home so sick. The second was now.

"What have we done?" they said to themselves. Dad did a double-take at my calf muscles which had been torn to shreds and doubled in size, Incredible Hulk-style, in just one week. The Lifeway Army training is designed to push you past your limits, into the arms of God. It was working.

The precious time with Roq flew by and all too soon it was time to head back. I said my goodbyes and cried all the way back to Lifeway.

After all, that which does not kill us makes us stronger.

The burden of suffering
seems to be a tombstone hung around our necks.
Yet in reality it is simply the weight necessary
to hold the diver down while he is searching for pearls.

Streams in the Desert, Julius Richter, July 9

14. A mission

2003

Boot camp continued back at base for two more weeks. Anything and everything could and did happen. The action kicked off with log-runs three kilometres up and down hills from Martins Bay to Lifeway with saturated logs so heavy you could hardly get them off the ground with three people. If we took longer than an hour we had to run the log an extra three kilometres down to the BP gas station in Snells Beach, and back up again, then do Martins Bay again until we came in under time.

We enjoyed mud-runs with the aforementioned logs, through the mangroves knee-deep in sludge, knowing that if we dropped the log we had to do press-ups in the muck. Whoever wasn't covered in muck from head to toe when we finished, had to get back in and get covered in muck from head to toe. It was hysterical. People pay good money for mud like that. This was where my brand new Asics were baptised, as I'd failed to heed the instruction, 'wear your mud shoes.'

We need to stop and acknowledge Singapore at this particular point. The Spencer Mak international incident involved the following factors; stinking swamp mud from A to B, slipping and getting tied up in, one electric fence, certain Mak family jewels, massive and recurring electric shocks to aforementioned family jewels and supporting structures, and never-seen-before biblically proportioned haematoma. Spencer endured the incident with a diplomacy and grace rarely seen on New Zealand shores. A good excuse to get out of PT? Probably not.

There were no problems with boredom as we tackled a wide variety of challenges such as pushing vehicles up hills at midnight, kayaking, orienteering, and more adventure-based learning games; each an epic story on its own. Amongst all this, the daily routine included PT twice daily, room-inspection, parade, drill, lectures, early-morning prayer meetings, and worship times.

As we listened to Trevor and Jan Yaxley speak, our eyes and minds were opened to what God can accomplish through a completely surrendered life. True-life stories that expanded our understanding of God even more were told in the very auditorium where one old man had one day toppled off his chair, and died while listening to Trevor speak. The cry for an ambulance went up. Trevor knelt over the man who had turned quite blue. He commanded the spirit of death to leave him in Jesus' name. Everybody watched as the elderly gentleman drew a big breath and came back from the dead.

One of the guest lecturers was Mal Maloney from Impact Ministries in Christchurch at that time. He had supported Lifeway with his teaching and ministry for over twenty years. Mal was a powerful teacher and was very knowledgeable in the area of deliverance or exorcism. He was a walking Bible, and all the powers of Hell knew it. Mal taught, and every student who wanted prayer was prayed for. The anointing was there to set people free by the power of Jesus Christ. A week before he came, some on campus and even the adjacent primary school became extremely twitchy, as many felt the impact of the Spirit of God.

And these signs will accompany those who believe: In my name, they will drive out demons; they will speak in new tongues. *Mark 16:17*

The Bible makes it clear that, as believers, we don't need a 'specialist' for this. All believers have this authority according to their faith, but it should be noted that there are also factors that hinder this prayer's being effective.

Unforgiveness, lack of repentance, and sometimes even lack of real desire to be set free. It sounds weird that someone might not want to be set free, but in some cases this is so. Deliverance would eliminate the only known (false) identity or set of excuses for not getting on with what one is created for. It should also be noted that deliverance can only be received by someone who has submitted his or her life to Christ, or the person could end up worse off than he was before.

> Then it goes and takes seven other spirits more wicked than itself, and they go in and live there. And the final condition of that person is worse than the first. *Luke 11:26*

Individual churches must take responsibility for their own in this respect, as the need is too great to be left to a few 'specialists.' The same goes for healing and evangelism; we all need to be doing it all. Mal wept as he told us of the angelic beings he saw on campus as he drove down the hill to Lifeway College on occasion. This was one of those occasions, and they were thickest near Trevor's office.

If you asked Mal a question, he would sometimes seem to quote almost an entire book of the Bible in answer off the top of his head. Scripture should always be the basis of ministry or counselling. His small frame, appearance and age reminded me of my grandfather, Pop. The similarities with Mal and my Pop didn't stop there — they had both been strong drinkers. Mal had been a Navy man.

One day God dealt with Mal as he lay on the floor of his friends' kitchen, fully conscious but incapacitated under the power of the Holy Spirit. When he got up a couple of minutes later (so he thought), three and a half hours had passed, and he was a very different man. He had met his maker, and after that, never touched another drink. During that time, God had healed Mal of a hereditary hiatus hernia, many demonic spirits and generational bondages, and most probably baptised him in the Holy Spirit at that point, while he was at it. From that moment on, Mal surrendered his life completely to God and his work. A few days later, the church elders came around to see what had happened and to pray for Mal, and that's when he began speaking in tongues.

Many were set free from family curses, soul ties and so on, and the way was cleared for learning and growing in God. I'd already had much prayer to set me free from Freemasonry, Celtic, occult, and witchcraft influences, but I still wanted to see whether there were any gremlins hanging onto me. Mal prayed.

"No, there's nothing demonic there. Hang on, there's an anointing here for you, so I'll impart that," his hand had started to shake on my head. "I'm not sure what it's for, but I can see you writing."

I thanked him, and wondered what on earth I would be writing. I had completely forgotten that God had clearly told me in 2001 that he wanted me to write my story, the one you're reading right now.

Lecturers taught on the nature and character of God, and received the first of our assignments. I was hungry to learn and so grateful to spend six months purely in pursuit of God. The group of people handpicked for each Lifeway Army intake was divine. I loved my new friends, and in hindsight, appreciated the ones who'd been put there by design to keep me humble and to build my character. Some of the very best and very worst times of my life were compressed into this six-month period, and at least five years of personal and spiritual growth.

However, it was a very confusing time for Roq, and a tough time for us all. At only three years old, Roq just couldn't understand why Mum had gone and left him. Every couple of weeks I made it home and we were both ecstatic. Roq would think I was home to stay, then a couple of days later we'd be saying goodbye, and our hearts would break again. Mum and Dad were left to deal with a very distraught small boy as I cried all the way back to Lifeway. I set my face like flint and settled it in my heart that I was going to give my best and get as much out of the training as possible, because it cost us so dearly. As usual, it was all or nothing.

And everyone who has left houses or brothers or sisters or father or mother or wife or children or fields for my sake will receive a hundred times as much and will inherit eternal life. *Matthew 19:29*

The weeks turned into months, and the end of the training drew near. Flab morphed into muscle. Comfort-seeking, self-serving layers melted away, leaving a raw desire for sacrifice, service, and self-discipline. Superficiality no longer sufficed. Earthly focus paled in comparison with things of eternal value. We learned the value of service. Thursdays were work days on campus. However, this particular work day we were sent out in pairs to serve the community. First up we were led by the Holy Spirit to ask a new, small business owner whether he would like some help preparing his premises. His eyes narrowed.

"And what do you want in return?"

We were so happy to say, "Nothing — it's totally free!", and see his cynicism turn to surprise and happiness. We worked clearing rubbish and sweeping for a couple of hours, and it made a huge difference to his day, and the preparation of his new shop for opening. The next place was a private residence. A beautiful elderly lady answered the door. Her face lit up when we told her we were from Lifeway and wondered whether she needed a hand with anything.

"Are you? I love Lifeway! My husband died there once and was raised again from the dead!"

"No way!" I said. "Was your husband the man who died in the auditorium the day Trevor was speaking and was raised from the dead?"

"He most certainly was!" she beamed and called over her shoulder, "Honey! There are some people here from Lifeway! They want to know if you need any help."

A darling elderly man appeared at the door, beaming. "Hello! Yes, I was raised from the dead at Lifeway. I love Lifeway. It would be great if you helped me with my sleep-out out the back."

We followed the careful steps that those old feet took to the small building he was renovating by himself. The feet that had walked through two World Wars and a depression. We sanded and painted with him, and marvelled at how the Lord works, and how he loves and looks after us. We were more blessed than anyone that day. It is more blessed to give than to receive.

Around the middle of our training we were sent out in small teams to different parts of the country to work with God's people, to bless, and bring about lasting change in people's lives. Sounds easy when you say it quickly. Our objectives over a two-week time frame were: work as a team, support ourselves, and make an impact on that community. My team went to Papamoa, in Tauranga, to work with a local pastor and help run a family fun day.

With God's grace and favour, we organised promotional material, games and events, and fundraised $5,000 worth of prizes from the generous local retailers for the fun day. Divine appointments flowed as usual, and we connected with many in desperate need of deliverance, encouragement, and a helping hand. We prayed for people, saw them set free of demonic strongholds in their lives, and given a new burst of strength to carry on. This was the first time I ever saw a person manifesting demons in front of my face, and that was just our team! Just joking, although as always, the dynamics of our team were challenging.

People we had not known poured their love and blessing back into our lives in a divine exchange. Our challenge became trying to pray big enough prayers, as it became clear there are no limits with God. As we served, we truly saw God supply all our needs more than in our wildest dreams.

And my God will meet all your needs according to the riches of his glory in Christ Jesus.
Philippians 4:19

I learned well the lessons of being flexible, always ready for action or change of plan, and not needing to know everything (or anything) ahead of time. It was incredible how much peace this new modus operandi brought to everyday life; of not knowing what the future holds, but simply, who holds it.

The chilly late September breeze brought the bronze leaves at my feet to life as I listened to the names being called. We were on the verge of a new challenge: Mission Possible, a tradition in the Lifeway Army training. This amazing, three-day event saw small teams sent out to accomplish a list of objectives, and to meet up at the appointed location by the set time. With no possessions to slow us down, we set off with God alone. No cellphones, ID, cash, credit cards, watches or changes of clothes.

The others were sent in threes in their groups, but we had four. Have you ever hitchhiked with four people? No one wants to pick up four people. Even if they do have room, which is almost never, they think "four against one, I don't think so," especially if one is carrying a long stick. I was walking wounded, brandishing a crutch after a bonus calf-muscle-blowout in a well-timed soccer incident. Our team were all New Zealanders: Shelly from Invercargill, Tim from Dunedin, and Hayden from Auckland.

Our provisions included two sandwiches and an apple each. We headed to the college gate to begin our mission. The other teams were dropped at covert locations to begin their most excellent adventures. Our envelope contained an audio tape and a list of objectives with further instructions. Hailing the first car that came along we rode into Warkworth with David Rippon, who had heard my story in church the day of my baptism. It's funny how our lives intersect sometimes, and we don't even know it. We put the tape in his tape deck and leaned forward, eagerly listening for the instructions. There was only one problem; it was in Japanese. The only words that stood out amongst the jumble were 'Gisborne', 'Napier', 'Taupo', and 'Matamata'. We needed to find a translator, and quick. One of our objectives was to get a written translation of the tape. With only three days to achieve our objectives, get to all those places, and be the first team to meet up at Matamata (we weren't very competitive), there was no time to lose.

We had to obtain a camera and take photos of each objective as it was completed:

- Catch an eel
- One team member to get a haircut
- Get a written translation of the tape
- One team member to pose as a mannequin in a shop window for 10 minutes
- Hold a PT (physical training) session with 5 strangers
- One team member to get a limb put in a plaster cast
- Serve a pastor of a church for 2 hours
- Mow a lawn
- Stay at a stranger's house one night and cook him dinner
  (a stranger who didn't know God)

- Sing a cadence outside a pub
- Get a photo of a team member handcuffed to a police car or inside a cell
- Get a photo of a landmark from each destination
- Get details of a Maori legend from a destination and re-enact it in front of the Army at a later date
- Get photos developed before arrival at Matamata (remembering we weren't allowed to take cash)
- Busk on a street and raise $10 (bring the money back)
- Give someone a bunch of flowers

Tim explained our mission to a kind lady in a Warkworth shop and showed her the respective paperwork. She gave us a camera so we could document our accomplishments, and a few minutes later I was taking Hayden's photo as he stood looking extremely guilty, handcuffed inside a police cell. We hitched a ride to Orewa and picked up a map. Hitching again, we were picked up by the chef from Lifeway College. He wasn't going our way, and didn't even like us, but turned around and made a special trip to drop us off at the Upper Harbour motorway off-ramp. It was late afternoon and the rain was pelting down hard enough to create flash flooding.

"Gee, I wish we could get a ride in one of those new Beetles," Shelly said, thinking out loud.

We were given dinner at Burger King at Upper Harbour; our offer to wash the windows was graciously refused, and we attempted to hitch a ride (yes, the five of us — Shelly, Hayden, Tim, Me and my Crutch) from the motorway on-ramp. This may seem obvious, but on-ramps are not the ideal place from which to hitch a ride. Everyone is in a hurry to get onto the freeway. Then again, anywhere in a city is not a good place from which to hitch a ride.

In spite of the challenges, one kind soul in his bank's company car let us squeeze our butts into his small-but-perfectly-formed red Volkswagen Beetle, ignoring the long line of people behind him tooting angrily and shaking their fists to get us moving. Shelly was stoked.

The Beetle dropped us off at Sky City Travel Centre in Albert Street.

Tim's stellar performance advertising our 'amazing race', and the favour of God secured us four complimentary bus tickets to Tauranga straight away. We happily snoozed en route and arrived in Tauranga around 10 p.m. The thought of sleeping on a park bench at the tail end of winter in a strange city weighed heavily on me as we walked up the road. However, a thought like that would never have occurred to Tim.

"So, let's find a hotel to stay in," came Tim's cheerful voice. Tim's God, I soon discovered, was much bigger than mine.

"Oh, of course," came my startled and slightly sarcastic reply, "a hotel!"

A few metres on from the bus stop, we spotted a sign saying '24 Hour Hotel.' Incredibly, we were given a room in this quality hotel to share for the night. No one was more surprised than me at the effortless provision of God, and the kindness of strangers. We were only limited by our faith.

The Lord is my shepherd, I lack nothing. He makes me lie down in green pastures, he leads me beside quiet waters, he refreshes my soul.
Psalm 23:1-2

We offered to work to pay for our room, but that wasn't necessary. In the morning, we breakfasted on fresh paninis, butter and grated cheese and date bakes from a downtown café, which we savoured in a beautiful garden on the waterfront in return for putting out some tables. We then visited Starbucks for a divine appointment. The girl at Starbucks knew a couple of girls from Lifeway and hooked us up with her friend across the street for a haircut, another objective on our list.

God was rolling out the red carpet for us so we understood that he would look after us much better than we could look after ourselves, if we let him. Tim stalked out of the salon, preening and perfectly coiffed for mannequin detail in a surf shop window for a full ten minutes. He really should give up his day job. He looked like a wax sculpture from Madame Tussauds', except he quickly changed his pose every few minutes without breaking character. His poker-face was remarkable considering we were standing out front on the street, laughing so hard the back of my head cramped up.

Check the photos on www.wildside.com.mx. He was legit.

God's divine appointments punctuated and brightened our trip all along the way as he touched people through us. We chatted with a guy on the street for half an hour and prayed with him for his needs. We had a lot to do and not much time, so Shelly and I went to get her arm in plaster, while Tim and Hayden split to get the tape translated. We regrouped with Shelly in plaster, but no translator was to be found. We were hungry again so we tried to earn a lunch at a couple of places. No one was interested in helping us.

"Stop!" commanded Timothy the Great. "God doesn't want to just give us any old scraps to scavenge off. We're His kids! What do we really want for lunch?"

"Well, I would really like Turkish," I said hopefully. I didn't even know whether there was a Turkish café in Tauranga, but would have killed for a Doner kebab.

"Ok," said Tim. "Let's go."

We set off and soon came across a Turkish café. We explained what we were doing, showed our letter as proof, and offered to clean windows in exchange for a lunch each.

"Oh, sure!" the man said, "You choose what you want. You don't have to clean windows," he said, graciously seating us at our table, and bringing us water. The lunch was divine. Thanking and blessing the Turkish café owner, we walked back out into the sunshine and regrouped. I noticed that I had that furry feeling so we went to the local dollar store and asked for four toothbrushes. To our amazement they gave us electric toothbrush sets and we got to freshen up, then tucked some fresh, God-given bus tickets into our pockets and we were on our way to Whakatane.

In Whakatane we busted a move to get straight onto a bus to Gisborne, but were refused. The sun was going down as we passed Pizza Hutt on the way out of town, and again the tummies were rumbling. It really is a hassle having to eat all the time. We looked at each other.

"Pizza?" We decided we wanted pizza for dinner.

At Pizza Hutt, we sang for our supper. With large sandwich-board signs we worked the footpath outside the store hard for an hour. Tim and Shelly put everything into a hysterical dance routine for the traffic. There were horns tooting, and lots of laughs. With bellies full of pizza and lemonade we headed on out of town with our thumbs out as the sun rolled over the horizon. Spotting a taxi driver, we asked him whether he would mind taking us to a place from which we could safely hitch, which he kindly did. Most cars that passed didn't have room for four extras, and the ones that did wouldn't stop. God was bringing someone special.

At last, he stopped. Our man was a survivor of the infamous Camp David cult in Waipara, Canterbury, where he'd lived for two years. He'd been a Christian for twelve years before that, and now happily called himself a Pagan. Sadly, he'd turned his back on God because of the failures of men. God, however, had never turned His back on him. Not even for one second. He was listening to Christian music when he picked us up, and he let us pray for him, which was by far the most significant thing.

We hit the road again and were picked up quickly by a lovely Maori man and his son who'd been white-baiting. We arrived at Opotiki right on dark. As we waited under a streetlight, a lady stopped who happened to be from Lifeway. She prayed hard core for us and then was on her way. Straight away a couple in separate vehicles pulled over and asked whether we wanted a ride. They had been to Rotorua and had just bought a new van with about ten seats. I had to laugh at the unlimited resources at God's disposal and the inventive ways he provided. He rarely does the same thing twice.

The Gisborne couple took us to their house and we cooked them dinner and stayed the night. Although they didn't know God, this lady was desperate to see God move in their lives, and was so grateful to have someone to talk to and pray with her. The man was a saw-doctor at the mill, who started work early, so we caught a ride into Gisborne with him in the small hours. After snapping our photo with the Gisborne sign in the freezing blackness of the early morning, we said goodbye and began to hitchhike. That was tough. We had finally struck the first really hard patch we'd had, and after several hours, our attitudes totally sucked. We walked and walked and walked. We'd gone over six miles when the familiar call came from Tim.

"Stop!" I was in no mood for a Tim pep talk, but it came anyway. I had a sick headache, missed Roq, and generally felt like crap. The honeymoon was over.

"Hey guys, we're not getting any rides because our attitudes really suck. We're not taking another step until we get it together."

With my feet splayed and back hunched, I dug my hands deeper into my pockets, stifled a growl and glared at the ground.

"Ok," he continued, as if I'd said, "Hey, that's a great idea!"

Tim launched into an Emmy award-winning, attitude-adjusting, gratefulness-declaring, team-building speech. It was a ripper that took at least ten minutes. By the end, I was sure I heard a triumphal musical score and saw mood lighting, which was followed by a prayer.

With Tim satisfied, we got the green light. I grudgingly admitted to myself that I felt a bit better. A couple of large, empty cars flew past, followed by the tiniest little hatchback car you've ever seen. I'd never seen one before, and I've never seen one since.

Reality merged into an animated children's movie. It was white, with large brown cow spots. It bounced past us, then screeched to a halt a couple of hundred metres up the road. A girl got out and ran back to see us.

"I'd love to pick you guys up, but I only have room for three."

Looking at the car, I thought she had probably meant room for two. It really was the tiniest car, and the entire hatchback and half of the back seat were crammed to the ceiling with clowning gear: a unicycle, cymbals and other crucial clown instruments and random stuff. It was jam-packed.

God had sent us a clown in a clown car.

"Please, please can we just try? Can we try to all squeeze in?" I heard myself begging.

She looked at me doubtfully. "Well, ok, you can try."

"Cool!" Shelly and I shared the tiny front seat. I was lying on my side with my arm bent around over the top of my head, following the line of the ceiling. My head was at a life-threatening angle while Shelly did battle with both me, and the gear lever. Tim and Hayden are not small guys and had a similar experience in the single available back seat. Every bump was agony. After two hours I was really ill, and just about to yell, "Stop! Let me out!" and jump from the car, at speed, and I don't get carsick.

"Yes, there's Taupo!" shouted the clown.

As soon as the doors opened, we erupted out of the clown car, which gratefully sprung back up a few inches. I was as white as a sheet. My common-garden headache had matured into a full-blown migraine, complete with nausea and trembling.

I shakily thanked the clown and we headed toward the Kentucky Fried Chicken store. Our timing couldn't have been worse: the lunch-hour had just begun, and there were people swarming all over the show. We approached the counter and bravely presented our letter and begged for some scraps.

"This is our busiest time," came the sharp retort. "Maybe we can do something for you if you come back later when it's not so busy."

We retreated. It was easy to fall back into old habits.

"Ok guys. What do we really feel like for lunch?" No prizes for guessing who'd said that.

"I feel like Valentines," said Shelly brightly. She's delusional, I thought. That's an all-you-can-eat buffet.

"I feel like spewing."

We started walking, and around the very next corner was a Valentines Restaurant. When we were over the shock, we went in and told our story. The lady was ridiculously nice.

"Sure, follow me!"

She escorted us to a waiting table and waved her arm expansively at the huge array of beautiful fresh food on offer. We were so grateful, and again offered to help with some jobs, but were told there was no need.

Once again we were stunned by the generosity of people, and the grace of God. Tim was right. It really did seem God wanted to give us the desires of our hearts.

From there, we made our way to the Napier Maori legend landmark and had our photo taken, ticking off the objectives on our list one by one. As we headed out of town, we came across a Trade Aid shop. This was the perfect place to busk and raise the ten dollars we needed for our next objective. We were given a set of ethnic drums and other instruments to play outside for a while. My head was still beating to the sound of its own drum. Predictably, the noise made my headache crank. In less than ten minutes, a kind man actually gave us ten dollars to stop playing. We didn't dwell too long on the implications, and the time for over-sensitivity had long passed. I think he was an angel and God was definitely having a laugh.

We walked to the bus station and tried to obtain some tickets to Taupo. It was not going to happen, but a guy gave us a ride to a safe location from which to hitch. After about an hour Tim and Hayden decided to make a sign saying 'Taupo or bust!' While they were away doing that, a large truck stopped, obviously thinking we were just two girls. When the guys came back at the same time as the truck stopped, he was sure it had been a set-up. Truckies aren't allowed to pick up hitchhikers, but he was kind and let us all squeeze in, even though he was convinced we'd tricked him.

The squeeze was again, very tight, and I began to feel very ill again very quickly. I hit a new personal low; the migraine became so bad I couldn't help crying from pain and nausea.

Halfway to Taupo our ride ended and my headache subsided while we waited for our next ride. Our morale was good and we had heaps of fun goofing around while we waited for our next ride. An amazing guy called Willie picked us up in his truck on his way to Taupo. Willie's truck had heaps of room for us all to be comfortable, and he even offered to share his motel room if we couldn't find another ride that night.

We decided we felt like a good steak dinner that night at Cobb & Co. The guy thought we were from a television show and called Lifeway to make sure we were legit. We could hear our leader laughing his head off through the phone. After an incredible dinner we found the bus station closed, so we prayed for guidance. We understood God said 'sleep', so we returned to Willie's room and crashed there. It was nice to have somewhere to freshen up a little before we left at 5.30 a.m. We thanked Willie, and headed directly to a big truck parked right opposite the motel, and greeted the driver sitting in the front.

"Could we possibly hitch a ride with you?"

"I'm waiting for my mate to turn up in his truck, and we'll roll together. I can take two, he can take two." And so they did.

God continued to make a way, where there was no way.

The Lord himself goes before you and will be with you; he will never leave you nor forsake you. Do not be afraid; do not be discouraged. *Deuteronomy 31:8*

We still needed ten dollars cash to get our film developed in Matamata, before we headed out to our meeting place at the farm. At the Taupaki Road turn-off we hooked another ride to Matamata with a man and his stepdaughter who was a real sweetie, and he gave us cash to get our film developed.

God gave us the breakfast of champions — hot pies. We had our photos developed, then found a ride to within a mile of the farm. We marched in formation and sang cadences as we approached, to finish well. We were the first group to arrive. We were ninety minutes ahead of our deadline, with fourteen out of seventeen objectives achieved, giving us second place in the points-based competition.

We were all winners on the day, however, and our view of our heavenly Father had changed dramatically. As we waited for the other teams, we watched a light plane begin to circle overhead, strangely appearing to wave at us with its wings.

"No way! That's Mike!"

It figured. It was Tim's friend. Mike's team had set their sights high and had been gifted two plane rides, a rental car and a cell phone. They'd been given $500 cash at an airport for one of their flights. They eventually pulled up at the farm in a taxi with some unbelievable stories. Team Nike all the way.

One by one, the teams came in. They'd all had amazing experiences and met some incredible people. God looked after everyone according to their faith. We nicknamed one of the teams 'Team Ghetto' because they hadn't asked for anything, and had slept on public toilet floors and in drains.

You do not have, because you do not ask God.
James 4:2

Life after Mission Possible was a major anti-climax. I had to come to terms with the fact that I had to support myself again, and knew I couldn't afford to live in the manner to which I had become accustomed. But it didn't have to be this way. It just took me a while before I could understand that I shouldn't have had such an adjustment to make. God really is my provider wherever I am, and living in the miraculous should be everyday life.

It's amazing how the simple things in life are so wonderful, and yet we can take them so for granted, missing them in the humdrum of life. A hot shower, our own bed, a nice meal. Rest. Family. We all looked forward to one or two of these.

Failing that, we have Psalm 23.

The Lord is my shepherd; I shall not want. He makes me to lie down in green pastures; he leads me beside the still waters. He restores my soul; he leads me in the paths of righteousness for his name's sake. Yea, though I walk through the valley of the shadow of death, I will fear no evil; for you are with me; your rod and your staff, they comfort me. *Psalm 23 (New King James Version)*

ೲೲ ೲೲ

15. The Kaimai's

2003

Once everyone had regrouped in Matamata from Mission Possible, we tramped up a mountain to a hut and were reunited with the packs we had packed before we had set off. After taking my share of the camping equipment and supplies, I discovered that my pack was so heavy I could barely stand, and scuttled out of control sideways, like a loaded crab. Luckily there had been no children or small animals in my trajectory, as they would have been steamrollered flat with no discussion.

'This must be a joke,' said the narrator, 'I'll just tell them it's way too heavy, and they'll take some stuff out for me.' But no, everyone's respective loads were the same. Bow-legged and almost bent in half, the test hike took us to the top of a mountain so high you can see 90% of the North Island of New Zealand from the summit. That night we put on a show, with each group re-enacting our best, worst and funniest times on Mission Possible, along with a skit of our Maori legends. After winning the prize for the best show, we were first up on the prayer roster that went all night. Each team prayed for an hour.

The next morning we were up at 5.30 a.m. After walking along the road for four hours just to get to the base of the Kaimai Ranges, we tramped for another nine hours, not counting breaks. When I hit a wall and felt I couldn't go on, I cried out to God to help me, and I actually felt someone pushing me up the hill. I looked to the person behind me, and thanked them for giving me a hand. He looked back at me blankly.

"I didn't."

For he will command his angels concerning you to guard you in all your ways; they will lift you up in their hands, so that you will not strike your foot against a stone. *Psalm 91:11-12*

We took a break for an afternoon PT session the first day, doing press-ups and running with our packs on. Once again I experienced the value in putting others first by encouraging and sharing when you're really hurting the most. It's a key that opens the lock to God's blessings. It's easy to bless and be nice when you're happy, and you've got plenty, but it takes real character to give your only chocolate bar away when you're in the middle of hell. And when you're in the middle of hell, don't stop! Keep going until you're out the other side.

That night after we made camp, we were in for a rare treat. Eight hours sleep, and no midnight challenges. It was just what we needed to set us up for another whole day of tramping, punctuated by impromptu PT sessions. In stark contrast to the 'do it to them before they do it to you' world, we worked as a team, doing press-ups with our packs on while we waited for the rest of our guys to catch up whenever we got too far ahead. No one rested until we were all together, leaving no man behind.

After a hard PT session that afternoon, we made camp in the bush and had dinner. That night we amused ourselves with tales of the unexpected about Mission Possible. A savage storm was brewing and was almost blowing our tents away already. We turned in, hoping for a good night's rest. Sleep waited and watched as I held onto the tent with a death grip the entire time, to stop it flying away in the gale-force winds.

Around midnight, the blower sounded. One minute to form up in our tramping gear.

"We're moving out. You've got twenty minutes to pack and form up!"

We tramped through the dense bush by torchlight until we finally came out along the road to Katikati, and stopped for a break at 3 a.m. We continued, but stopped often to do press-ups and sit-ups. Every time a car came along we crawled into the drain to avoid being hit. I fantasised about staying in the drain while they carried on without me, but my feet kept going, one in front of the other and the waking nightmare just didn't stop. We dozed in and out of sleep or consciousness with our eyes open.

And we walked, holding on for dear life to the only thing we had to hold onto, and the only thing we needed.

Whoever dwells in the shelter of the Most High will rest in the shadow of the Almighty. I will say of the LORD, "He is my refuge and my fortress, my God, in whom I trust." *Psalm 91:1-2*

At 6 a.m we stopped on Hot Springs Road in Katikati for an hour break, the fastest hour in recorded history.

"Break's over! Gear up ready for PT with your packs on!" came the call.

My feet were so injured they felt like mincemeat, with a spongy layer of plasma in between the mince and the skin. I could barely walk once I stopped. But walk we did for another hour, not knowing when it was going to end. Not knowing we were on the last road.

As we had wanted to give up just metres from the hut at boot camp, the temptation to give up on the last road was overwhelming. Kat Afoa sat down on her pack and cried. She was done, and refused to go another step. However, love never fails, and a little encouragement and a smile gave Kat the strength to carry on. Then came a bolt from the blue.

"Listen up! This is the last road, and there are hot springs at the end where we can have a swim. Then we head back to Lifeway. Well done."

In the space of one hour, we had made a quantum leap from hell to heaven. Who knew, I would even find some energy for a few celebratory back-flips, having again found the will to live. We had tramped over sixty miles, up and down mountains in two-and-a-half days with heavy loads and killer PT sessions right off the back of Mission Possible. Never in my wildest dreams could I have imagined that I would ever accomplish something like this. And if not for God, I couldn't have.

Most of us were taken back by vehicle, but there were a raggedy few who couldn't fit in, so they hitchhiked the 240 kilometres back to Lifeway. This mission was the gift that just kept on giving, and they were up for it.

Back at Lifeway we had just sat down to a good feed, the first in a while, when the call went out.

"You're leaving for your Wilderness Solo. You'll be in the bush for three days on your own. Be formed up in half-an-hour in clean hiking gear. Pack water, sleeping bag, roll mat and pen and paper."

Firstly, at approximately thirty-six chews per bite it was going to take me at least half an hour just to eat my dinner, and secondly, I had hiking gear, but I certainly wouldn't call it clean.

Our supplies for the solo consisted of a couple of squares of one-ply toilet paper (whether we needed it or not), three snack bars, two bananas, an apple, and an orange. Luxury! We were given the makings of bivouacs, a square of plastic and some bailing twine. Some had tents already set up for them. We'd been shown to our spots by torchlight, and most had to make our own bivouacs. Once I had mine sorted I burrowed into my sleeping bag, yanked it up over my head and down over my eyes. The drawstring pulled tight around my face left just an air hole for my mouth. I was in manatee mode and went into hibernation until further notice.

Come to me, all you who are weary and burdened, and I will give you rest. *Matthew 11:28*

I was about as happy as I could get while gale force winds, rain and hail once again raged around me. I was glad that my bivouac blew away while it was still light and I could fix it properly. Carrie Moulden had rats fighting on the roof of hers, and others were flooded out. Sienna's blew away in the middle of the night. That was all fine, but the spider bite that made her eye swell shut, not so much. Sienna stormed out of the bush the next morning in a cloud of expletives, shouting something about 'jamming it somewhere'.

The three-day solo was cut short as the blower shattered my precious sleep. If I never hear another one of those blowers again in my lifetime, it'll be too soon. We were called in early because of the storm, to my great disappointment.

We can do so much more when we draw on God's strength than we can on our own.

My grace is sufficient for you, for my power is made perfect in weakness. *2 Corinthians 12:9*

Graduation had finally arrived and the survivors had not just survived, they'd thrived. We dressed for the occasion and headed to the auditorium. Mum didn't recognise me, such had been the transformation that had taken place: she walked past me on the stairs. I was a different person in every way than the one she had known. The extreme outer transformation was an accurate reflection of the inner one. Sam was there for me too, along with her beautiful kids to help celebrate my graduation. Roq wasn't well and was at home with Dad. The Principal of Lifeway College called up the graduates one by one and presented us with our hard-earned certificates, to the applause of an enthusiastic crowd.

It was a big day. God smashed a familiar lie that I'd always held to be true, "I'm average, that's all, average." Ok, but not quite good enough. And I had to work hard to achieve average. The whole training I'd worried I wouldn't be able to handle the academic work and would fail after all that because I was out of my league in a tertiary institution. Now everyone was going to know I was average. Fearing the truth of it, I over-compensated, working ruthlessly on my written assignments and handing in pages and pages more than were expected or needed.

I accepted my certificate with sincere gratitude, but God wasn't finished.

" ... and because of the diligence shown in your assignments Janet, you have also won the Principal's Award," said the Principal. He seemed to talk for ages and I zoned out and went into shock. After what seemed like long enough, I tried to snatch the gift he held out to me so I could slink off the stage, but he resolutely held onto it until he'd finished speaking, so we were stuck in a strange tug-of-war. Trying to get a grip on myself, I calmed down and tuned back into what he was saying.

" ... and I always enjoyed reading your work." And with that, a long-held false belief was smoked. God's truths about us are very different from what some of us believe about ourselves. Once we find our identity and strength in Him, nothing is impossible *(Luke 18:27)*. A wise man once said, the only limits we have are those we place upon ourselves.

It's sad that many of us are held captive by false belief systems that stem from a single event, a cruel word, or a childhood of abuse, and we become defined by them, unable to reach out further than the bars on our minds, to see that they're not even true, but when the Son sets us free, we are free indeed *(John 8:36)*.

I had been brought into a new place, a very spacious and beautiful place. The old had passed away and the new had come, but our journey with Jesus is a process and will not be complete until he comes back. In the meantime, I press on, and God still deals with me one issue at a time.

These are just the broad brush-strokes of my training, but you get the picture. Even the stories I seem to have gone into great detail to describe are still only a rough overview. The spiritual and emotional groundwork that took place was by far the most significant aspect, yet I haven't really touched on this. Those who are interested will find more in my next book, 'A Table in the Presence of my Enemies,' amongst other things.

My Lifeway Army training was the best and worst of times, a crucible for refining character, and only for those who have or want a surrendered heart and a willingness to move forward. In an environment like that, issues come to the surface quickly and can be dealt with, and ground is gained fast.

As the training drew to an end, I was now ready to learn.

He is wooing you from the jaws of distress to a spacious place free from restriction to the comfort of your table laden with choice food. *Job 36:16*

Even after graduation, the training didn't stop. We still had a few more days together to keep tweaking our attitudes and expectations. It challenged what it is in us that wants to slacken off when our noses are turned towards home and as the finish line comes into view, and we learned to finish well. It was a fun camp and a bonus half-marathon seventeen kilometre run to round things up in the now intense summer heat.

This was hard, as I was now frantic to get back to Roq. The most difficult part of my training hands-down was our separation. As time had worn on, understandable anger erupting from Roq's primal wound had begun to cloud our visits. Little did I realise that being reunited with Roq was to be a different sort of boot camp altogether.

I returned to my dorm room and looked at the boxes piled up. I was all packed up but had nowhere to go. I'd been frantically looking for a place to rent in Snells Beach for the last couple of weeks, but all my efforts had been met with closed doors. The real estate agents were never there when I went to see them and I couldn't get hold of them on the phone. Everyone else around seemed to be getting sorted and finding flats. But not me!

"Do you trust me?" asked God.

"Yes."

"Well, trust me then."

"Ok, I'm leaving it up to you."

I stopped actively looking and found peace because I had given it to God to sort out. Peace in the knowledge that he had the perfect place, empty and waiting just for us. Peace in knowing that the blessings he had for me no one could steal, and in that I took great comfort. It would be a dream come true to have a place to call our own. The day before I had to leave my dorm, my friend Barbara happily told me about her new flat. I was happy for her, but she noticed the disillusionment in my eyes about my own situation.

"Don't worry. It will happen for you too," she said. "Have you talked to Lynley? She had a flat available at her place," and she handed me the phone number. Fast forward several hours and I sat crying with gratitude in my perfect sunlit, three-bedroom flat that had been sitting vacant the whole time I'd been knocking myself out searching. I had a need of a bed, lounge suite and a fridge. The flat was empty apart from a double bed, lounge suite and a fridge, and there was no agent's fee to pay. He's a last minute God because he needs to teach us how to trust him, and I was glad I had.

My new landlady, Lynley Smith, was a friend that I hadn't met yet. Journalist, teacher, grandmother, adventurer, and author of the non-fiction book From Matron to Martyr.

Just as God had said, he had blessings for me that no one could steal, and he has them for you, too.

A father to the fatherless, a defender of widows, is God in his holy dwelling. *Psalm 68:5*

I signed up for Active Duty and was available for being sent anywhere in the world God chose to send me. But he knew what we needed was security and stability. This was the sanctuary Roq and me called home for nearly six years and the backdrop where Roq grew from a hurt and angry little boy into a strong, courageous young man.

For a while, Mark had Roq for weekend visits with most fortnights. Roq loved his Dad but was terrified of his tattoos and couldn't bear to look at Mark at all if he had short sleeves or a singlet on. I continued to let Mark take Roq for weekend visits even when Roq was screaming over Mark's shoulder, "DON'T LET HIM TAKE ME, MUM!" just so I could say, "Well he can't say I didn't try," as many single mothers do. For some single mothers, it is ok. But it wasn't for us. Not then. In fact I had been too soft in this regard, allowing access even after it was clear it wasn't working, people-pleasing to Roq's detriment.

After the deadline for Roq's return was missed one day, I was encouraged to gain legal sole custody and have only supervised visits, which I did. It was hard for Roq to come to terms with the fact that his Dad, despite his good intentions, just wasn't in a place himself where he could be the father Roq needed at that time. It didn't mean Mark loved him any less.

Many hours of counselling were called for to help Roq work things through. The search for the right counsellor was another battle, but one worth fighting, as it was to be funded through a government agency. I stated my preference for a Christian counsellor, but was told these were very rare and we would need one that was approved, and I'd be best to just go with the one they put forward. In good faith, we went along to the interview, but I had a bad feeling right from the start. After a few minutes of conversation God intervened. He wasn't having any mistakes made with his boy.

"… and would you like me to address the spiritual aspect of Roq's therapy?" the counsellor asked.

Shocked, I asked, "Oh, are you a Christian?"

"No, but I can still attend to Roq's needs on a spiritual level."

"I'd prefer you didn't," I said firmly. That was the deal-breaker. Then, just in case I hadn't got the message, the strangest thing happened. The ground actually shook like an earthquake was happening.

"Wow," I said looking around. "What was that? Did you feel that shaking?"

"Ah, no, I didn't."

I had felt it loud and clear. I had been warned.

"Well, thanks for your time, we won't be going ahead with any sessions for Roq, thanks anyway," and couldn't get out of the place quick enough.

I was still pressured to accept the counsellor that was presented, but stubbornly refused to go ahead. I stated my desire to source my own qualified, certified Christian male counsellor, and off I went. It was a process, but eventually I found a wonderful male Christian counsellor for Roq who was literally a godsend. He gave Roq a fantastic set of practical tools to use in situations in which he was struggling, and helped Roq change the belief that he was 'bad'. This was the start of Roq's healing from fear, rejection and anger, although it was a long road, being also inextricably tied to my healing and behaviour.

For a while, I was 'the enemy' in Roq's eyes, stopping him from seeing his Dad, even though he was terrified when he did. I learned that sometimes you just have to be the bitch. Once I'd come to terms with being the bad cop, I set my face like flint and prepared myself for whatever fallout was necessary to keep the ship on course. I understood Mark's pain, but it was hard being accused of not caring, and of not finding it hard and of not feeling any pain of familial separation when nothing could have been further from the truth. This was one of the bitterest blows because it had been, hands-down the hardest thing I'd been through apart from losing my brother, and I had grieved bitterly. I had waited for Mark for years, but it didn't matter. It doesn't matter how well people know us, they never really know what we are going through. There's only one who does.

I knew the truth, and in the end I refused to let accusations affect me; I learned what it means to let the peace of God that transcends all understanding guard my heart and mind *(Philippians 4:7)*.

I learned that it doesn't matter what people think but only what is true; and to stay true to God, my son, and myself, and at all costs.

The emotional fallout Roq had to deal with was one thing; the spiritual damage was quite another. By November 2005, Roq and I had been spending time every second weekend at Mark's house having supervised visits. I discovered that we had both picked up a hitchhiker, the spirit of death. Mine was spotted and dealt with at church, and I asked God to help Roq be set free also. I explained to Roq about how God had got rid of the spirit of death from me.

"I have that. Can you get rid of it for me?" he said, clearly speaking divine wisdom at five years of age.

It was an answer to my prayer. Roq had been struggling more and more with anger, rejection, fear and shame. Worse, he had asked several times to "go home" (to heaven), a shocking thing to hear come from your little child's mouth. I prayed for him in the authority and name of Jesus, and he was instantly set free.

There were still many layers of spiritual pollution that needed cutting off; and open doors that needed closing. These were things that had come down the bloodline, freemasonry, the sins of the fathers, and I was still going through this process myself. I hadn't understood fully yet that Jesus has done it all, that once we're hidden in Jesus we're free from everything and those things had no authority over me anymore. I still struggled with demonic visitations, night terrors, and nightmares.

It took years to make all those mistakes, and it took a fair while to fix them. Often I would be just on the verge of sleep when I would hear a bloodcurdling scream from Roq's room just like Mum and Dad used to hear coming from mine. I'd race in, ready for anything, and see Roq jumping up and down on his bed in absolute terror, hands over his ears and his eyes following some unholy creatures flying around the room. He could see things I couldn't see. I had seen so much evil, my spiritual skin had become calloused.

It was at these times I was most grateful for the gift of tongues — the heavenly language — the language of the spirit. It was automatic and was used for any purpose God needed at the time, worship, intercession or warfare. It worked.

The Son is the image of the invisible God, the firstborn over all creation. For in him all things were created: things in heaven and on earth, visible and invisible, whether thrones or powers or rulers or authorities; all things have been created through him and for him. He is before all things, and in him all things hold together. And he is the head of the body, the church; he is the beginning and the firstborn from among the dead, so that in everything he might have the supremacy. For God was pleased to have all his fullness dwell in him, and through him to reconcile to himself all things, whether things on earth or things in heaven, by making peace through his blood, shed on the cross. *Colossians 1:15-20*

His name is Jesus Christ.

16.  The Shofar

2004-2014

For many years, we were set apart from those we love while we healed and forged a new place to stand. Through many tests and breaches of our new boundaries, we realised the significance of personal boundaries for our emotional and spiritual wellbeing.

I served a year deployment as part of the Lifeway Army training at Family Television on the campus of Lifeway College. Roq attended the neighbouring Christian school and I stayed on at Family TV for another four years doing graphics and video editing. Personally, I was railing against being single, battling with a strong need for a husband and father figure for Roq. A word came for me from God through the boss's wife, Lauren Henderson, one day.

> **"Nothing is going to happen for you in that area until you accept Jesus as your husband. And when you've accepted Jesus as your husband, then you will be like royalty to him."**

So that became my quest — to find out how to accept Jesus as my husband. I asked God to show me what that meant, and over time he showed me what that looked like.

"In that day," declares the Lord, "you will call me 'my husband'; you will no longer call me 'my master.' I will remove the names of the Baals (false gods) from her lips; no longer will their names be invoked. In that day, I will make a covenant for them with the beasts of the field, the birds in the sky and the creatures that move along the ground.

Bow and sword and battle I will abolish from the land, so that all may lie down in safety. I will betroth you to me forever; I will betroth you in righteousness and justice, in love and compassion. I will betroth you in faithfulness, and you will acknowledge the Lord."
Hosea 2:16-20 (brackets, mine)

Now that's what I call a husband. Whenever I felt lonely or longing I would consciously turn my attention to Jesus instead of to people. I imagined myself holding his hand while walking down the street if I felt alone and it never failed to bring a smile to my face. I talked to him about family issues like a wife would talk to her husband, and he was faithful to sort them out.

"He's your son! You sort him out," I would say to Jesus in my heart.

"I will. You just stay out of it." And he would sort it, and do a better job than I could too, and still does.

For over a decade, my birthday had been the saddest day of the year for me when I was with Mark. He 'didn't do birthdays.' But God restores the years the locusts have eaten *(Joel 2:25)*. In 2011, we were living in Snells Beach and we visited the folks in Ruawai on my birthday. There was a visiting prophetic team from Bethel School of Supernatural Ministry in the United States at Ruawai Community Church that day. No one knew it was my birthday. One of the girls pointed me out in the congregation and prophesied over me.

"This day is for you — your birthday is special. Jesus is your husband,

and he is walking down the aisle to meet you."

I was weeping in the presence of the Lord and couldn't stand up straight. The prophecy kept coming and coming, but I couldn't hear. Jesus was here to see me! I had never experienced that much voltage before. It seemed even more intense than when I was baptised in the spirit. I tried to pull myself together. I didn't want to miss any more.

"You are a mother to nations. God is going to answer your prayers and give you the desires of your heart. You need to dream bigger."

From where I am standing now, I look back and realise by God's grace I have been single and abstinent for well over a decade. Jesus is my husband, and I feel like royalty — and nothing else matters. Now I walk up to him in spirit; we smile, and he scoops me up in his arms and whisks me away to paradise. He loves me no matter what I do and gives me the grace to avoid intentional sin. He never lets me down and never leaves me. He laid down his life to purchase my eternal life with him. And yours.

Now that's what I call a love story.

♦♦♦♦

In August of 2004, Steve Thompson and a prophetic team from Morningstar Ministries visited Lifeway College from the United States. I rustled up Carrie and another mate, Andy, and I took my seat between them in the auditorium. The team began to pick people out of the audience and speak the prophetic words the Lord had given them. I was pointed out and stood up, to my great discomfort.

"God has given you the heart of a counsellor..."

Unbelievably, I interrupted the guy mid-prophecy with the most inane of remarks.

"That would be right — I'm a loser magnet!"

Carrie and Andy gave me filthy looks and tried to move away. Steve Thompson turned to a team member and said, "What did she say?"

"She said she's a loser magnet," and they all cracked up laughing. When we recovered, the prophecy graciously continued.

"Ah yes, the heart of a counsellor, and a heart for seeing restoration in your family. God has given you the gift of openness in your life and people find you very approachable. The Lord uses you for a channel for his goodness and power. Many have been touched. Isaiah 61:4 is also for you."

> They will rebuild the ancient ruins and restore the places long devastated; they will renew the ruined cities that have been devastated for generations. *Isaiah 61:4*

The next day, I bumped into Steve in the dining hall. "I couldn't believe what you said. It nearly killed me," he said, laughing.

"I couldn't believe what I said either. I'm such a dork."

If God can work through someone like me, imagine what he can do through you.

> But God chose the foolish things of the world to shame the wise; God chose the weak things of the world to shame the strong. *1 Corinthians 1:27*

One of the ways in which God was going to work through me was through my story, but for a long while it wasn't time to start. Then it was time, but it was too overwhelming. I fought with God that I needed a laptop, even though I had a desktop set-up. He gave me a laptop. I tried to get the story going, but didn't know how to do it. I asked everyone I could think of for help, but just got more and more bamboozled and intimidated. Story-arc, character development, knowing the ending first; the more I found out, the less I knew.

God just sat back and watched. Then, his still small voice said; "Did I tell you to go around asking people for advice, or try to find someone to do it for you?"

I stopped. "No, you told me to write my story. But I don't know how. It's too hard!" I wailed.

"Do you remember when you were at Lifeway and everyone used to love hearing your stories?"

"Yep."

"Well, just write your stories out, and I'll weave them together with you."

"Oh ok," he made it sound so simple. I wasn't convinced, but it was a place to start.

After a few false starts I finally found a rhythm that seemed to work. In my spare time while, at Family TV, I got the first half of this book drafted down. As I grew more and more burned out, I had to become disciplined to keep it moving forward. I gave myself a goal to write for at least an hour before going to sleep at night. Because I was always trashed by the time I fell into bed, I would have to trick myself into getting started by saying, "Just open it up and have a look. You don't have to do anything." Or, "Just do five minutes." As soon as I opened up the file, thoughts and ideas came straight away, and I'd generally get more done than I expected. In between full-time work, home-life, church, miscellaneous and family dramas, laptops dying, and projects for friends, this story began to take shape.

One night in bed, tired, but writing, I heard the Lord say, "You should stop now and pray. Do some spiritual warfare. Do it now."

I could feel dark forces gathering, but I was on a roll and it was easy to shrug off the still, small voice. I carried on for another hour or more writing Chapter 4 about the visitor in the tattoo studio. If you managed to get through that chapter, you'll understand what I'm talking about. The enemy of my soul was not happy, and he wanted to shut me up. He sent out an assignment against me. All of a sudden I really needed to go to the toilet. All of a sudden I was aware I should have stopped and prayed when I was told. I was overwhelmed with a fear so thick I could see it. I had to stifle a scream as I ran to the toilet and lunged for the light switch. When I flicked the switch, the light bulb shattered, and the glass cascaded to the floor. My scream could be contained no longer, but was soon replaced by speaking violently in tongues that sounded so harsh it scared me even more. I raced to the CD player and got my favourite worship music on as quickly as I could. I cleared the glass and put a new bulb in, but it was at least two hours before I started to calm down. But things still weren't right.

The next morning I was sitting in the lounge when Roq got up and headed to the toilet. He rocketed straight back out with his eyes bugging, trying in vain to hide his fear. I'd been trying to teach him not to be held captive by fear — that we have authority over it, but this time I understood. There was definitely an issue from the night before.

"What's the matter?"

"Nothing."

Shortly afterwards I met my friend Sharon Thorburn, founding director of Kotuku Rising choir, New Zealand Queens Service Medal Recipient, Winston Churchill Fellow, ordained minister, teacher, singer, songwriter, composer and grandmother.

Straightaway she said, "Oh, I can't stay here. We'll have to get Lynley and pray together, the three of us. A cord of three strands is not easily broken," *(Ecclesiastes 4:12)*. Lynley arrived and pray we did. We anointed the doors, windows, pillows and mirrors with oil and the cleansing power of the Holy Spirit, commanding everything to go that was not of God, in the name of Jesus the Christ.

Sharon saw in the spirit that my 'third eye' was open, and that's not a good thing. If only I'd been obedient and prayed for protection when God told me while meditating on those ungodly memories. My life is one vertical learning curve and one of my life purposes is to warn people. This was something I didn't know about, but here's what I've found about opening the third eye.

The occult is knowledge of secret or supernatural powers beyond the range of ordinary senses, or secret/hidden information only available to the initiated. The third eye (or inner eye) is a psychic ability connected to the occult. This metaphysical opening refers to the sixth chakra (brow) that leads to 'higher consciousness', and is a new-age symbol of enlightenment.

Meditation, or the emptying of one's mind, as common in eastern cultures, opens us up to the spirit realm and achieves an altered state of consciousness. It is the doorway to all metaphysical activity. Christian meditation is the exact opposite, and means to think or dwell on scripture or the things of God the creator (not deities people refer to as 'God'), until a deeper meaning is revealed through the Holy Spirit. The 'emptying of one's mind' for extended periods of time is not recommended, as the law of physics demands, a void must be filled. God will never force himself upon a person without their consent, so that leaves only one other who will fill that void, uninvited.

Those using yoga as a means of enlightenment engage meditation, forced breathing patterns and unnatural positions to force the kundalini, or serpent power, at the base of the spine upwards to the crown chakra to bring enlightenment, characterised by light and a state of bliss. However, even yoga professionals advise that this must be done with careful and proper preparation otherwise it can lead to insanity or even death. That is because serpent power is not from God the creator, but from the one who comes only to steal, kill and destroy.

> Jesus came that we may have life, and have it to the full. *John 10:10*

Buddhists refer to the third eye as the middle eye of Shiva, Hindus refer to the eye of clairvoyance and wear the Tilak, or red spot between the brows. In Egypt it's known as The Eye of Horus or the Eye of Osiris. In Freemasonry it is the All Seeing Eye in the pyramid, the same one that is found on the US dollar bills. Whatever the flavour, the eye usually means the same; esoteric knowledge that man so desires, and the passing into a spiritual world that we have no business entering, unless we are in Christ.

We need to be very careful to eat only from the Tree of Life and not the Tree of the Knowledge of Good and Evil.

> For God knows that when you eat from it your eyes will be opened, and you will be like God, knowing good and evil... then the eyes of both of them were opened. *Genesis 3:5-7*

The pursuit of enlightenment outside of God is detestable in His eyes, and leads only into the dark realm that masquerades as light. Make no mistake: God doesn't want us to be ignorant or 'unenlightened.' That's why he gave us Jesus, the Bible and the Holy Spirit. In God's economy, enlightenment is called wisdom and revelation, spiritual discernment, words of knowledge, visions, and dreams, just to name a few, and in these things God is the ultimate all-knowing, all-seeing authority, who gives his gifts and wisdom freely.

If any of you lacks wisdom, you should ask God, who gives generously to all without finding fault, and it will be given to you. *James 1:5*

ෂෙ ෂෙ

It was all go on every front as usual, and this particular moment in time at work saw the birth of a design and production company under the Family TV umbrella. As time went on my role took more of a project management tack but encompassed over-flow design work when required. It was an incredible and testing time, working alongside a great team, but my lack of professional boundaries meant that, over time, I suffered burnout.

As things grew more out of control in my work life I became horribly stressed and tired, and the effort of keeping my happy/capable mask from slipping too far only added to the load. Being quite incapable of quitting, as usual, I'd given myself permission to die trying, and Roq was pushed more and more to the sideline.

This only compounded Roq's insecure bond with me caused by my inconsistent emotional and physical availability to him during his life so far. His ambivalent attachment style meant that he needed me desperately, but I terrified him. He was terrified of my absence, terrified by my occasional but nasty anger issues, and terrified of being disappointed anymore. He tried his utmost to be the best boy so I wouldn't leave him again, but when he lost it, his tantrums were out of this world, as was his need to be the boss. Combine well with two very strong-willed personalities and the recipe had nuclear capability.

Once again, God intervened. An intensive fourteen-week Christian parenting course, 'Growing Kids God's Way', gave me crucial tools and wisdom. Over time, as Roq saw consistent improvement in my behaviour, he began to trust me. But I was still horribly overcommitted at work.

One day when I was stressed at work I saw the hurt in his eyes as I snapped at him for asking if he could go somewhere and play. I saw that Roq had accepted in himself that I was too busy for him, and that was fair enough because work was important, and he was not. Something in me finally woke up and screamed, "No, that's not true, and this is not ok!"

Most of the communication we'd had over the last couple of years was in the form of my barking orders so we could get everywhere we needed to be on time to keep things together. It was all I could do to hold my mouth closed as I dragged myself around the house doing endless housework on my time off. There was no time or energy left for life. With growing economy of words as my strength faded, at times my communication had reverted to a base level of one-word sentences... "COME"... "HELMET"... "TEETH"... "BED."

Oh, God, forgive me! This was a brutal realisation. I was responsible for letting the dry rot of over-commitment multiply unchecked in our lives. I thank God for the low-points that are painful catalysts for positive change, for opening my eyes and once again, for rescuing us.

One day at work I started crying and couldn't stop, and this was no ordinary day. It was the first day back at work after the Christmas break. I was supposed to be rested, refreshed and looking forward to the year ahead. However, I found myself quivering with anything but anticipation. The low cloud of depression had moved over me so slowly I hadn't become conscious of it until Dad pointed it out.

I had no choice but to hand in my resignation at the soonest possible moment, if not before. I had finally got off government assistance and was supporting our little family, an achievement I was proud of. This meant another terrifying step into the unknown.

I fessed up to Roq and apologised for failing him. I told him that he was much, much more important than anything else in my life, and asked his forgiveness. Roq sighed a very big sigh and shrugged his little shoulders and said simply, "It's ok."

Such grace from such a small boy, and his eyes reflected a shift in understanding. He was allowing himself to believe and trust it would be different now. God smiled.

Now I had to walk it out.

God is not disillusioned with you,
because he had no illusions about you in the first place.

I remember the saying, "Time is money!" Well that is simply not true. Time, is in fact, a lot more valuable than money because it is an unrenewable resource. It's amazing how a good thing can slowly turn into a bad thing when balance and perspective have been lost. Great weariness of soul is an indicator. The people we love beginning to droop and sag around us, is an indicator. Health issues and feelings of hopelessness and depression are indicators. How blind we can be to the consequences and casualties the lack of balance and boundaries can bring.

It's a wonderful thing to step back and take a good look at the priorities in our lives from time to time with our families, with our King. There has been no greater reward for the hard calls than to see joy return to my son's countenance and to enjoy time with him. Even to this day, quality time remains very important to Roq.

Never let us be discouraged with ourselves;
it is not when we are conscious of our faults
that we are the most wicked: on the contrary, we are less so.
We see by a brighter light. And let us remember, for our consolation,
that we never perceive our sins till he begins to cure them.

François Fénelon (1651-1715)

In 2009 after six years in our first flat together, Roq and I moved to a beautiful little house near the water down the other end of Snells Beach. We had room to move and grow and a stunning natural playground on our doorstep. My bedroom was upstairs on a mezzanine floor with an incredible view of the bay and Kawau Island. The tall ship the Spirit of New Zealand visited the bay often and you could see the splashes when people had their early morning swims. Orca and dolphins played in the bay. God gave me a new view, new vision, and the courage to dream again.

As usual, it was a little rocky at the start. Even though we'd blessed the place, there was a bad feeling in the house. I felt like I'd taken a kick to the guts and my stomach ached constantly. Roq was totally bound by fear and our beautiful rabbit Tabetha Bear had turned into a feral beast. We didn't know what was wrong, but God did. After a couple of weeks, Sharon came to visit, stopping by on her Footprints of Hope walk of the entire length of the country to raise hope and give hope. As soon as she walked into our new home in her walking shoes and high-visibility vest, she knew something was wrong.

"Wait, I need to get my shofar," and off she went.

"Your *what?* You have a chauffeur now?"

A shofar is a Hebrew trumpet-like instrument of ancient origin made from a ram's horn. Used in spiritual warfare, its sound is said to pierce the heavens. I'd never heard of it. There are many things I don't understand, but I discovered the issues with that end of the beach were two-fold. It had been an area of terrible bloodshed during Maori wars, and it was close to the entrance of Snells Beach and an active coven. A gateway.

When you go into battle in your own land against an enemy who is oppressing you, sound a blast on the trumpets. Then you will be remembered by the Lord your God and rescued from your enemies.
Numbers 10:9

Sharon returned and took the magnificently long, curved ram's horn from its velvet case.

"Every time the shofar is blown it gives a different sound. The sound changes to accomplish what God needs it to do in each instance," Sharon said.

We went upstairs to my room and faced the stunning bay. The shofar blew and the call went on for what seemed like ages, far longer than Sharon had breath. The sound was pure, powerful and unique. It touched my soul and scattered the powers of darkness around us. The spiritual ripples went out and out from it, and I knew it was indeed reaching the heavens. It was the sound of God's victory over sin and death. It was the sound of authority. It was the sound of sacrificial love. And I wept and wept.

In Roq's room, the shofar blew. The sound was very different from the sound in my room, a lot higher, and shorter. Things were different after that. Peace descended upon the house. Fear had fled. My stomach ache had disappeared, and our adorable Tabetha Bear was herself again.

> In this world you will have trouble. But take heart!
> I have overcome the world. *John 16:33*

❧ ❧ ❧

Still, God continued to lead and guide us. Roq had been baptised at eighteen months with the support of his godmother, Leslie. I had explained to Roq as best I could, but wasn't sure how much he understood. The little man was not to be underestimated. With a cheeky two-tooth grin he had lifted up his t-shirt to show his tummy and said happily, "God in tummy."

When he was four, Roq had been listening to me praying for family and had interrupted.

"You've got to pray for me too!"

"Do you want to have Jesus come and live in your heart?"

"Yes!"

Roq beautifully prayed the prayer of salvation with me, was born again; and heaven rejoiced.

> The children of your servants will live in your presence; their descendants will be established before you." *Psalm 102:28*

Roq was now ten; and God prompted me to ask him whether he wanted to be water-baptised to strengthen his commitment to Christ. Roq was keen and I made arrangements, but he decided he wanted Sharon to baptise him at Snells Beach. The timing was perfect. Sharon was to come and rest up a bit with us after she finished her Footprints of Hope walk. We pampered the shredded feet, laughed and marvelled together at who God is and what he does. Sharon emerged from the bedroom the next morning after what I'd hoped was a restful night's sleep.

"Well, I feel like I should be exhausted after last night, but I actually feel like I slept."

"What do you mean?"

"God dealt with me all night last night. I don't know whether I was awake or asleep, but it was as though I was watching a video of my life relationships and issues play out before my eyes. God showed me things. It's important he work through these things in my life so I can baptise Roq."

On the 17th of January 2010, the family gathered for the special day and watched from the beach as Roq, Sharon and I waded out into the bay. The presence of God was with us and Roq came up smiling from his baptismal dunk.

"I had a word from God for Roq," Sharon said after we had prayed. "But I don't know if I should say it because it's a bit of a weird one."

"Go on."

"I heard the Lord say, 'His sword shall pierce the darkness.' That means he will be in darkness if his sword is to pierce it."

"Well, that's life isn't it, but there's a great promise there."

The light shines in the darkness, and the darkness has not overcome it. *John 1:5*

Roq and I finally said goodbye to Snells Beach when God called us home to Ruawai in April of 2011, the land of milk and kumara, to be close to family and to finish Take a Walk on the Wild Side.

It is a wonderful thing to be living in absolute freedom and to be able to laugh at the past. It is a wonderful thing to experience the ultimate freedom that came from forgiving the man who killed my brother. It is even better to be doing what I was created for in life. I've discovered Maslow's box is not the authority on happiness, as it is plain for everyone to see — just look at Hollywood for example. Success, fame and living your dreams doesn't automatically guarantee you happiness. However, finding salvation and purpose in Jesus does, whether things go well or whether they don't. Happiness is no longer dependent on circumstances, but is an integral part of me that nothing can take away for long.

> The rain came down, the streams rose, and the winds blew and beat against that house; yet it did not fall, because it had its foundation on the rock. *Matthew 7:25*

DL Moody once said, "Our greatest fear should not be of failure, but of succeeding at something which doesn't really matter."

Am I doing Christ's sacrifice justice with how I'm living my life and the time I've been gifted? This poignant and challenging question helps to keeps me on track, as I live on while others have died. I was bought with the highest price heaven could muster. My life is no longer my own.

Because of that, today my cage is gone. My hope and future lie in hands that know no limits. The same hands that created the plan for my life even before he wove me together in the secret place, even before the foundation of the world.

Do not settle until you've found yours. Take a walk on the wild side with Jesus.

> The ransomed of the Lord will return. They will enter Zion with singing; everlasting joy will crown their heads. Gladness and joy will overtake them, and sorrow and sighing will flee away. *Isaiah 51:11*

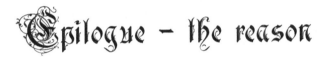 Epilogue – the reason

Eternal

Mum stood at the kitchen bench and looked out over the fields towards Matakohe Cemetery. Tears welled in her eyes, streamed down her face and dripped steadily into the sink. A question swelled in her heart. Her question was the precursor to the vision that started it all for me eighteen years later.

"What's the purpose of life? What is the point in having children, to lose them just like that? What is it all about, God?"

God heard the cry of her heart, and answered her in a way that was precious and unique to her alone. He showed her that he was real. He took her by the hand and they began an intimate journey of revelation and relationship together. He gave her a rock-solid faith in the living God. He took her ashes and gave her his beauty in return, the divine exchange. He took an unspeakable tragedy and made it count for something. Something huge, that involved the healing of a generational line and activated destinies.

I've discovered the answer to my burning question about the meaning of life. We came from God (not monkeys — well most of us, anyway), were made perfectly equipped to fulfill the purpose for which we were created — to worship and glorify God with our hearts, lives and the gifts he has given us; and to spend eternity with him. The only problem is, since the fall of Adam, the sin ceiling tends to get in the way of our communication. God is holy, and we are not, until we take up the righteousness Jesus offers.

No matter how good we are or are not, we are all sinners, every last one of us. For all have sinned and fall short of the glory of God *(Romans 3:23)*. The wages of sin is death, but the gift of God is eternal life through Christ Jesus our Lord *(Romans 6:23)*. But God demonstrates his own love for us in this: while we were still sinners, Christ died for us *(Romans 5:8)*.

The gospel means 'good news', and the good news is that your sins and mine have been paid for at the cross. You are the apple of his eye; the reason he lived and died and rose again.

We can't earn salvation by good works or deserve it by having good character. If this were the case, Jesus would have died for nothing. God offers it to us freely. All we have to do is receive it by faith. If we confess with our mouth, "Jesus is Lord," and believe in our heart that God raised him from the dead, we will be saved *(Romans 10:9)*. Everyone who calls on the name of the Lord will be saved *(Acts 2:21)*.

If you're ready to take a walk on the wild side, ask the same question I asked. The one that Jesus is leaning forward, just waiting to hear you say, even if only in your heart:

"God, if you're real, show yourself to me."

You've got nothing to lose and everything to gain. If your heart is beating faster than normal, and you just know that you want Jesus to be the Lord of your life, pray this one:

"Lord, I surrender my life to you. Come into my heart. I ask forgiveness for my sins. By faith I receive the gift of eternal life. I ask that you baptise me with your Holy Spirit and with fire. Thank you for setting everything right between you and me. Show me the way forward with you, in Jesus' name, Amen."

Congratulations, you've just made the most important decision of your life. Now ask God to show you a good church to be a part of, and to bring the right people around you, and he will. The best is yet to come.

God sends no one away empty
except those who are full of themselves.

DL Moody

ABOUT JANET

I am a daughter of the Most High God; rich beyond measure, daily receiving every blessing the mind of God can conceive, and I wish this for you too. I serve a limitless God; I just wish I could stop placing limits on myself. The challenge: surrender more, obey quicker, dream bigger. I would rather be at the bottom of Maslow's box with God; than at the top without him. My heart beats to encourage and inspire.

I still like to rebel. I rebel against the culture of this world, and the boxes people try to put us in — to love when it says to hate; to give when it says to take; to abstain when it says to indulge; to be faithful when it says to betray; to be pure in an obscene culture; to honour when it says to criticise; to serve when it demands endless selfies; to crave silence amidst the clamour of a million voices. To hate sin but to love the sinner. In other words, to be more like Jesus; or to die trying… some things never change. And to not beat up on myself when I fail at all those things.

To be wise, not enlightened; to see the miracles in the mundane; and most of all, to be thankful. I love to write about the things that matter, and to encourage seekers to find the truth that will set them free, which stands high above the quagmire of deception that we call 'enlightenment'.

I stand on the verge of a new story, hand-in-hand with the man of my dreams that God has chosen for me after thirteen years of being alone, and no friends with benefits. My new husband. He's royalty in God's kingdom. I was almost paralysed with fear and unworthiness when I realised who he was. But the Holy Spirit reminded me of his promise — that when I had accepted Jesus as my husband, I would be like royalty to him. So we stand together, humbly in love in front of our Lord with joy unspeakable in our hearts.

I would absolutely love to hear from you. Check out some photos, and leave a message on the website. You are welcome to drop by the Take a Walk on the Wild Side Facebook page and connect with other Wild Siders.

Thank you, and be blessed to be a blessing.

The beginning.

None of the rulers of this age understood
it, for if they had, they would not have
crucified the Lord of glory. However, as
it is written: What no eye has seen, what
no ear has heard, and what no human
mind has conceived — the things God
has prepared for those who love him.
2 Corinthians 2:8–9

www.wildside.com.mx

www.facebook/
takeawalkonthewildside